SPIN Works!

SPIN Works!

A media guidebook
for communicating values
and shaping opinion

Robert Bray

Robert Bray, Author, Editor and SPIN Project Director
Don Hazen, Managing Editor and Executive Director,
Independent Media Institute
Seeta Peña Gangadharan, Associate Editor
Judy Hong, Editorial Coordinator
Robyn Wexler, Copy Editor
Tamara Straus, Editorial Consultant
Designed by Nigel French, Small World Productions
Cover and Artwork by Kimberley West
Energy and Ideas by Holly Minch

SPIN Works! and the efforts of the SPIN Project are made possible by the
generous support of the Albert A. List Foundation, Arca Foundation, French
American Charitable Trust, Jessie Smith Noyes Foundation, McKay Foundation,
New World Foundation, Solidago Foundation, and the Unitarian Universalist
Veatch Program at Shelter Rock.

**Published by special arrangement with the
National Gay and Lesbian Task Force Policy Institute**

Table of contents

Section 3: Moving the message .37

Section 4: Reacting to media 87

Section 5: Media and community 97

Resources 109

Index 121

Acknowledgments

SPIN Works! is the result of years of experience and the generous contributions of many supporters and participants. We are thankful to the community activists who contributed their expertise and case studies to this book so others may learn from them.

We are extremely grateful to those who paved the way before us in our struggle to make this a better nation by making its media more responsive to the needs and concerns of its people. We honor the work of activists everywhere who toil to give voice to the unheard and leadership to the marginalized. This book is dedicated to you. We appreciate media watchdogs who help hold the media accountable. We are grateful to the hundreds of journalists we've worked with over who still believe that the media has the power to transform society and shape our lives for the better.

I would like to give special thanks to Don Hazen, executive director of the Independent Media Institute (IMI), who believed in the SPIN Project from the beginning, provided management and oversight to this publication and continues to champion the noble concept that a strong participatory democracy is best served by a strong, inclusive media.

Special credit goes to Seeta Peña Gangadharan for her editing and writing skills, persistence, intelligence and for being the "glue" that held everything together.

Also, thanks to the staff of the SPIN Project and the Independent Media Institute, in particular Holly Minch, Judy Hong, Tate Hausman and Erika Wudtke. My appreciation is extended to the board of IMI for supporting my work and strengthening the independent media. Robyn Wexler and Tamara Straus copyedited the book superbly and Nigel French designed it creatively. Kimberly West artistically created the cover and other art. Christine Triano and Jeff Gillenkirk helped with the writing and fine tuning.

I am especially indebted to the program managers, directors and board members of the foundations that support the SPIN Project, in particular Christina Roessler and Diane Feeney, French American Charitable Trust; Marjorie Fine and Deborah Holder, Unitarian Universalist Veatch Program at Shelter Rock; Colin Greer, New World Foundation; Rob McKay, McKay Foundation; Millie Buchanan, Wilma Montanez, Victor De Luca and Stephen Viederman, Jessie Smith Noyes Foundation; Steve Cobble and Eric Sklar, Arca Foundation; Diana Cohn, Solidago Foundation; and Allison Barlow and Helen Brunner, Albert A. List Foundation. A warm, heartfelt thanks to Jane MacAlevey for her leadership in making the SPIN Project happen in 1997.

Thank you to my family for ongoing support and understanding. Lastly, I offer loving, personal thanks to John Church, married to me and the movement for 10 years and going strong.

Special acknowledgment to the National Gay and Lesbian Task Force

This guidebook is published in a special cooperative effort with the National Gay and Lesbian Task Force (NGLTF). NGLTF has been a major influence in my political and professional life, as it has been for many gay, lesbian, bisexual and transgender people who have struggled and continue to struggle for their civil rights. As a former NGLTF media director I have been the beneficiary of the talents and wisdom of its staff and board. The oldest national gay rights group in the country, NGLTF has a strong foundation in progressive social change. Its mission informs my writing of this book. In particular, I would like to thank Kerry Lobel, NGLTF executive director; Sue Hyde, who constantly creates change all around her; and all staff past and present who lay their lives on the line for queers everywhere. Most importantly, I want to thank Urvashi Vaid, NGLTF Policy Institute director, the brilliant, passionate force of nature who helped rescue me from corporate America and set me on the progressive course I follow today.

—Robert Bray

Introduction

Note from the author

Welcome to SPIN Works!, a media guidebook designed to give you the nuts and bolts of effective public relations and media activism. It is a collection of activist-friendly information: case studies, models for success and tips designed to make all of us better media spin-meisters and -mistresses.

The word "spin" often has a negative connotation, and indeed it should. Much of what passes as "news" today is the well-greased and highly financed public relations propaganda of corporations, politicians and right-wing operatives, designed to sell us something we do not want from sources we do not trust, whether it be a product or a policy—or sometimes both in one.

I would like to reclaim the word.

Spin is not only the acronym of our project—**Strategic Press Information Network**—it is something we must all do better. For me, spinning the news is not about pulling the wool over someone's eyes or manipulating information in a dishonest manner. It is about framing our news, moving our messages and proactively engaging the press in a way that is respectful of reporters while aggressively presenting our side of the debate. The days of waiting for the phone to ring from reporters are over. It is now time to take our news out to the world.

I am a confessed spin-a-holic. Press conferences constantly play out in my head. Soundbites are always on the tip of my tongue. I dream about media events. Extreme? Possibly. But I believe when we champion our case to the media—when we spin our news—we actively:

- Shape public opinion on important issues.
- Spark debate.
- Influence policy.
- Capture attention for our organizations.
- Create change for people we care about.

I have had almost twenty years of professional media experience in both the corporate and non-profit political worlds. When I think back on that time, two moments stand out for me—moments that changed the way I thought about the power of the press to communicate my beliefs and values, and to shape my own identity and future.

Both have to do with my work as an activist in the gay, lesbian, bisexual and transgender civil rights movement.

The first occurred in 1987, in front of the United States Supreme Court. At the time I was a junior public relations executive with the IBM Corporation. And a big closet case. Nobody knew I was gay

other than myself and a few close friends—not my family, not my co-workers, and certainly not my high-level bosses at IBM.

All that changed in an instant because of the media.

I had taken the day off from IBM to volunteer to handle the media for a huge gay rights protest in Washington, D.C. Standing in front of a phalanx of cameras and microphones at a press conference I helped to arrange, I came out to the world over network television.

It was an accident, really. I was killing time and directing reporters' inquiries to official spokespersons. One network television reporter, who knew me from the corporate beat and IBM, asked for some kind of comment "on the record." I broke my own rule of "never wing it." *(See "Dos and Don'ts" page 16.)* I looked straight into the camera and said: "Hi Dad. It's Robert. I'm gay and I'm proud and I love you."

Slightly sentimental, possibly cheesy and definitely "off message." But I said it. And the reporter used it. Thinking back, I can see why it was used: It fleshed out the story with a personal element.

Suddenly, I was part of the news and was being quoted on national television. My family, tuning into the TV that evening by coincidence, saw me come out. My boss stumbled upon the segment while channel surfing. Millions of people saw it, hundreds of whom found a way to contact me and tell me their own coming-out stories.

I would never be the same after that soundbite. I quit my yuppie IBM job six months later, joined the gay rights movement and came out officially to my family and friends. It put me on a path of political media activism I follow to this day. The power of the media to transform my life and the lives of others was made loud and clear in a very personal way.

The other example of the media's power to change me took place a few years later at a press conference I produced at the National Press Club in Washington, D.C.

The issue was hate crimes based on sexual orientation. I myself have been attacked three times, so this issue was personal. A courageous man and designated spokesperson, who had survived a horrible gay bashing/murder in Houston, Texas that killed his lover and crippled him for life, stood up in front of a wall of cameras and reporters, waiting to speak. Also in attendance were politicians sponsoring the Hate Crimes Statistics Act, which was before the U.S. Congress at the time, and various hate crimes activists and law-enforcement authorities seeking its passage. The bill was stalled in the

House of Representatives because of arch-conservative opposition.

The experts and politicians at the press conference line-up gave their statements. The reporters dutifully took notes and listened to all the statistics. Then it was the survivor's turn. He got up in front of the world and openly cried for his lover. "How could this happen to me?" he agonized. "I loved him…and they killed him. They killed him because he is gay. Why won't the government take action to stop this?"

I could see the cameras zooming in for the close-up. I could see the hard-boiled capital press corps leaning forward in their seats, some of them clearing their throats from emotion. And in my mind I could see tomorrow's headlines—along with the photos, captions, charts, soundbites and strategic media-messages. We were already booked on "Larry King Live."

The bill passed the next Congressional session. It was the first piece of legislation in American history to affirmatively include homosexuals. I was invited to the White House signing ceremony. Standing a few feet from then President George Bush, I remembered how we had spun this story right into the living rooms and consciousness of the American people.

Did the media pass this bill and change policy? No: It came about because of years of hard work by national and grassroots activists. But the media certainly helped to change how many people—including policy-makers—felt about hate violence.

And it changed my life.

All of us who work for positive social change in the many struggles we wage—civil rights, economic justice, environmental justice, reproductive freedom and health, immigration, affirmative action, welfare and others—have stories to tell to the media. These are stories and messages that communicate our vision of how we want society to treat us.

And that is the purpose of this book: To give you the resources and skills to move messages that make a difference, inspire, galvanize and give voice to the silent.

We must better learn how to tell our stories and advocate for our issues through the press. This will directly affect how people feel, think and vote. That is spin. And we are spinning for our lives.

—Robert Bray

What is the SPIN Project?

The SPIN Project provides technical media assistance to nonprofit public-interest organizations across the nation that want to influence debate, shape public opinion and garner positive media attention. SPIN offers public relations consulting, including comprehensive media training and intensive media strategizing and planning.

SPIN stands for Strategic Press Information Network. We are growing the capacity of organizations to get their voices heard and do more effective media work on issues important to the future of our society. The project was created in January 1997. It is housed at the Independent Media Institute, a nonprofit organization located in San Francisco.

We believe the time is now for organizations to boldly engage the press and communicate their values and frame their issues. We want to help people make their voices heard. We seek a stronger democracy in which people can enhance the public discourse and actively participate and live to their full potential. This is what drives our work at the SPIN Project.

The SPIN Project works with a broad range of social policy, advocacy and grassroots organizations, all of which are working to strengthen both democracy and public participation. They typically focus on issues concerning civil rights, human rights, social justice and the environment. SPIN honors the multiracial, multicultural, diverse constituencies of the groups we train. We consistently work with people of a wide range of ages, sexual orientations, ethnicities and incomes.

We travel constantly, training and strategizing with organizations in the field. Annually, SPIN covers tens of thousands of miles, training hundreds of people as we travel from state to state. Our work has taken us from *barrios* to boardrooms, from Native American reservations to national activist conferences in major U.S. cities.

For more information contact us at:
SPIN Project
Independent Media Institute
77 Federal Street
San Francisco, CA 94107
(415) 284-1427
E-mail: info@spinproject.org
Visit our Web site at http://www.spinproject.org

Navigating this guidebook

In your hand are more than 100 pages of information and almost two decades of experience that will help you work better with the media. We have divided the book into six sections: an introduction and five sections. There is a natural "arc" to the guidebook in terms of using it, starting with building a strong foundation of planning and strategizing and then adding specific media tasks.

The **Introduction** sets the big picture, contextualizes your media work in the larger arena of democracy, the media and progressive social change values.

Section One provides the basics, with which all media activists should familiarize themselves before embarking on higher-level media work.

Section Two is about honing messages, framing issues, being good spokespersons and other tasks that should be realized before you reach out to reporters.

Section Three is about reaching out to reporters to score news. In other words, "moving the message" proactively, as we say in the PR business.

Section Four details how to hold media accountable.

Section Five is an examination of how media activism changes communities.

Finally, the **Resource section** offers dozens of media groups, publications and related organizations that will be of use to readers.

Sprinkled throughout are case studies, tips and checklists. Activists should feel free to duplicate these lists and use them in the field or when planning your media.

Several topics are cross-referenced for elaboration (for example, see *"Photo Ops"* and *"Staging Media Events"*).

As the book emphasizes, it always makes sense to start with a foundation—setting your goals, targeting your audience, framing your issue, constructing your messages—before building on that foundation with a media plan and communicating the message through the press. That, in essence, is how this guidebook is constructed.

Who is *SPIN Works!* for?
What will it teach you?

Engaging in aggressive, proactive media work requires a significant commitment of an organization's resources and a step up in its public profile. This guidebook is designed to provide tips and resources to help national and local groups maximize their media potential.

SPIN Works!

✓ Is for those groups that can absorb intensified media scrutiny and responsibilities. If your organization is fledgling, has a delicate infrastructure or an impossibly overworked staff, you probably should hold off on doing media work until you are internally stronger.

✓ Is for those community activists willing to work with the media—not against it. Despite our frustration with the media—especially in terms of who is quoted, what news is covered, what viewpoints are expressed or left out and what we perceive as its biases—this guidebook is designed to give you resources and skills to engage the media in a respectable manner.

✓ Is for community advocates with news to make. Do not waste reporters' time with non-news. Have a story to tell and be newsworthy.

✓ Emphasizes the importance of treating journalists, reporters, producers and other news figures with the utmost professional respect. Most reporters are decent people highly trained in their craft who practice a rigorous set of journalism ethics. This does not mean you cannot constructively criticize a reporter and respond to negative coverage. But it is important to be a helpful resource for reporters—not an adversary.

✓ Is low-budget, high-impact media activism. Most grassroots groups using this guide probably do not have fabulous PR budgets to finance high-gloss media campaigns. You obviously will need some money to pay for the phone bill, photocopying and so forth. But for the most part this is "$1.99 public relations"—albeit PR with principles.

✓ Emphasizes that media work does take resources and certainly requires planning. It is critically important to incorporate media strategy into your program and fundraising plans. Strong, do-able media plans are the key to successful media work.

✓ Presents information keeping in mind how a reporter thinks. If you understand how reporters think, what their editors demand, and how news is reported, you can do a better job convincing journalists of the importance of your story.

✓ Highlights the fact that there is no "magic media bullet." It is never possible to predict precisely what reporter or media outlet will go for a story, if any. Even with the best plans, you may not make the news. Do not take it personally if your story gets bumped. It happens. Try again, because SPIN works!

Out of the salons and into the saloons

Jim Hightower

As an everyday yakker on AM talk radio across the country, I run into the slippery little conundrum of communicating a progressive message to a mass audience on a near-daily basis. And from my experiences as a practicing populist politician, the challenge is not delivering your message to the bean sprout eaters, but to those snuff dippers out there as well.

So, how do we start talking and quit preaching? Three quick tips come to mind:

Numero uno: Mr. Humor is not our enemy. Indeed, he is our friend. So be not afraid of Mr. Humor. He is there to open doors for us, to open hearts and maybe to even open some minds. So when he arrives in your head, do not reject Mr. Humor. Yes, it is of course serious business that each and every one of us are engaged in. And yes, indeed, it is a grim world out there. But hey, nobody likes a grouch.

Whether your humor is broad and bodacious, or dry, sly, wry and petite—whatever you've got—turn that little sucker loose, please. I commend to you my own personal credo: You can fight the gods and still have fun. After all, we are engaged in the glorious work of taking on the powers that be on behalf of the powers that ought to be. And we need to enjoy that.

Tip number two: Know what it is you want to say. What is your message? And by message I don't mean that full truckload of information and issues that you want to dump on the American people. Instead, what does it all boil down to? Say it so folks can get it—get it in their hearts, get it in their guts—because that is after all what truly motivates each and every one of us. Certainly does me.

In my mind, our progressive message boils down to a small set of big values—indeed the founding values of our people and our nation. Very, very radical values. Economic fairness. Social justice. Equal opportunity for all people, and good stewardship of this globe. There are hundreds of issues represented by our organizations, but I dare say that they'll fit within this framework of values. Values the American people already hold deeply within themselves, and cannot be shaken even by the money and the media power of the conglomerates in our society.

Let's take one issue as an example: economic disparity. Because there is so much economic disparity in our land today, a lot of progressives want to talk about redistribution of wealth. My advice?

Please don't. A phrase like "redistribution of wealth" is policy wonkishness at its worst. It sounds like sex talk for economists. I'll tell you how I would try to communicate this issue of economic disparity. Indeed, let me give you a six-step recovery program to heal the heartbreak of wonkishness.

Jim Hightower
Radio Commentator
Hightower Radio
Box 13516
Austin, TX 78711
(P) 512 477-5588
(F) 512 478-8536
(E) hightower@essential.org
www.jimhightower.com

Step number one: We're not really talking about redistribution of wealth; we're talking about economic fairness. We're talking about the value of fairness, expressed something like this: "The workaday majority of American folks, working harder and longer than ever before, are producing greater wealth than ever before and getting less and less in return. That is not fair, pure and simple." That's what's in the hearts of every American in the United States.

Step number two: OK. You've established the values so now you can take a small step toward wonkishness. You can attempt to put a number to document this unfairness. Not too much, just a little bit.

It can sound something like this: "Wall Street likes to boast that the '90s are a time of unprecedented growth and prosperity, yet 80 percent of us have lost income. Eight out of 10. It's not just the rich versus the poor anymore; it's the rich versus the rest of us."

And then you can take one more little wonkish step and say: "In the past decade we, the American people, have generated $12 trillion in new wealth. What have we gotten out of that? What is our percentage of that, that eight out of 10 majority? We got just one percent. That divides out to less than keeping up with inflation, which is why we're falling behind. The rest of it went straight to the top."

Step number three: Here's Mr. Humor knocking. Now is the time to rivet this unfairness with a memorable punctuation point. I'm partial to the zinger, to the one-liner, something like: "Sure, Wall Street's whizzing. It's whizzing on you and me." People get that. Or maybe a pop culture reference. Instead of some long quotation from Goethe or Nieztsche, why not Ray Charles? He's good. He had a song that said, "Them that's got is them that gets, and I ain't got nothing yet." The American people know that in their own experience. You do not have to explain it to them.

5

Step number four: Now is the time to personalize the unfairness. Personalize it; put a face to it. "How many people do you know who made $100,000 last year? Less than five percent of the American people make that much money, but one who did is Mikey Eisner, the head Mouseketeer of Disney, Inc. In 1995, he made $100,000. Not for the year, not for the month. He didn't make $100,000 a week; he didn't make $100,000 a day. He made $100,000 *an hour.* Plus a car. Meanwhile, he was knocking down the health care benefits to the minimum-wage workers at Disneyland and Disneyworld." You get it, right?

Step number five: It's time for Mr. Humor again. Another zinger, something like, "Some of these executives like Michael Eisner, they're getting so rich they can afford to air condition Hell. And the way they're acting, they'd better be setting some money aside for that project."

Final step, number six: Put a tag on the unfairness. Something like this: "Economists have a technical term they use to characterize this transference of wealth from the bottom to the top. The technical term is 'stealing.' Faster than a hog eats supper, they're stealing from us. But the real term for what's happening is 'class war.'" See, now we put *our* term to it: class war. "The privileged few are waging an unrelenting, take-no-prisoners class war against the middle class and the poor people in this country; and it's time we begin to fight back against it."

Having achieved this six-step program, you can *now* be wonkish because you have folks' attention. You've set the stage for the solutions that you want to discuss, from living-wage campaigns to third-party politics, from taxing the stock transactions of the elites to fighting for the re-chartering of American corporations.

Believe in yourself. What you want is exactly what most Americans want. We want our country back. We want it back from the greed-heads and the deadheads, from the speculators and the spoilers, from the bosses and the bankers, from the big shots and the bastards who are running over us. And that's what America wants. That's what ordinary folks want.

Say that to the people. Say it plainly; say it again and again—as widely and as loudly as you possibly can. Get the biggest microphone you can possibly grab, and say it again and again. And then smile.

Smile. Not only will the workaday folks in this country—the workaday majority—understand and appreciate your smile and what you're saying; but that smile will also drive the powers that be absolutely crazy. Of course, that's a pretty short ride for most of 'em.

Commentator Jim Hightower's Chat 'n' Chew program is broadcast on more than 100 stations across the country. You can hear the show on the World Wide Web. Go to www.jimhightower.com.

Who owns the media and how it works

Don Hazen

Most of you know the bad news about the mass media: Virtually all major media are owned by global or national media corporations. Network TV and affiliates, cable TV, commercial radio, daily newspapers—most of the media operating in your community are likely to be part of chains, with headquarters far away from your community.

Coverage

Partially as a result of the consolidation of media into a handful of huge companies who control much of what is seen, heard and read, our media system—especially TV—is increasingly dominated by infotainment, fluff and violence. The media system is well known for its ability to scapegoat people and blame victims for social problems. Historically, and even today, the image of whole groups of people—people of color, union members, gays and lesbians, young people, to name some—can often be distorted by the corporate media.

As large corporations take over media companies once locally run as family businesses, there is often more pressure on profits and the bottom line. That's one reason why you often hear about journalists and media workers losing their jobs and a reason why coverage has become more superficial and violence-prone.

It is also true that it is increasingly difficult to get coverage of social change issues—in other words, to get your message out. Infotainment has become a media staple. On your local TV station, weather and sports take up greater amounts of air time. Very little time is allocated to public affairs on TV—a recent study cited local TV stations that have no public affairs programming at all—and the time devoted to commercial advertising in a given half hour of TV or radio has steadily increased over the years.

Discouraged, but...

Yes, it is easy to get discouraged by the state of our media system. Corporate media plays a tremendous role as gate-keepers. They decide what is important, what is news, and whose voices will be heard. I do not want to fool you. Your job to promote the issues of your organization—to help keep hope alive for your constituencies—will not be easy. But then most things worth doing are not a breeze, right?

It is possible to have a significant impact on your local media. In fact, if you are smart and hard-working and you apply the skills and knowledge contained in this book, some success is almost guaranteed. There are thousands of success stories—examples of grassroots groups and advocates persuading the corporate media to tell their story in a way that helps their cause or meets your objectives.

Don Hazen
Executive Director
Independent Media Institute
77 Federal Street, 2nd floor
San Francisco, CA 94107
(P) 415 284-1420
(F) 415 284-1414
(E) dhazen@alternet.org
www.alternet.org

Contradictions in the system

How is success achieved? Like all large systems, corporate media has contradictions. First of all, understand that the corporate media system is completely dedicated to making money from advertising. The media system delivers you—the consumer—to the advertisers. That is why network TV and many newspapers are free. There are now commercials even in movie theaters, schools and museums, as the tentacles of advertising spread throughout public space.

Entertainment, news and information are used as a lure to get your attention and deliver you to the advertiser. Even on public television, programming is frequently shaped by what corporate advertisers will pay to get on the air and commercial messages—or sponsoring credits—are getting longer and more elaborate.

Credibility

Yet, because media companies need credibility with their consumers, they cannot just put propaganda on the airwaves. In newspapers and magazines the standard for coverage is often considerably higher than it is for TV and radio. Your local media has a responsibility to your community to give some semblance of fairness and cover a wide range of activities. That is where you come in—to firmly request that your issue gets fair coverage along with the others.

Journalists and producers are good people

There are many good people working in journalism who believe the media's positive role in making democracy work. Hiring good and competent people is part of the media's effort to gain public credibility. Media companies often hire people with reputations for being fair and sensitive to human issues. That they often try to control those people or their material is another story. No doubt you will have an experience with a reporter or a producer who blames the fact that the story did not get in the paper or on air—or often how it is framed or headlined—on the editors: the "higher ups," the ones you rarely get a chance to have contact with.

Another problem can be self-censorship. As ambitious people want to be successful in media companies and move up the ladder, they often will decide not to publish a story—sometimes without even testing it out, for fear their bosses will not like it (even if the editors never say that outright). Of course, there are some highly publicized situations where stories are outright killed because senior staff do not want them.

Public mistrust

Many polls show the public is tremendously mistrustful of the media. According to a poll taken for the Freedom Forum, almost nine out of 10 people felt that advertisers have too much influence over the news and news coverage. For a lot of people, the media industry is as unpopular as lawyers and politicians. Many news consumers are turned off when the media insists it is being objective in its coverage, for people know that to be untrue. People feel the media should be more up-front about their biases and not lay claim to a super-human, absolute objectivity.

Large media companies are aware of these problems and are working to improve them. A whole area called public or civic journalism has emerged over the past decade—mostly in newspapers, but in some cases in TV and radio coverage. The idea is to get the media and the reporter more involved in helping to address community problems or to provide deeper or special coverage of vexing issues like racism or corruption. Some people think civic journalism is more a PR gesture, while others think it is an authentic effort on the part of media companies to better meet their responsibilities in their communities. You will have to decide where it fits in your community, if your local media has embraced this concept. The point is that media companies are feeling vulnerable and it is up to you to leverage this situation to help your group or your cause.

Another potential tactic for garnering coverage is taking advantage of the fact that a given market is often shared by different companies. Sometimes TV networks compete with one another. It is especially possible to get radio and newspapers, for example, to compete with and sometimes even criticize TV and other media. While pack journalism is prevalent—often covering the same thing and sticking to tried-and-true formulas—sometimes you can get good coverage from one media outlet because it wants to show up another one. Or you may discover agendas at play that you had not even known of that can land you good publicity.

Keeping your composure

In the media world there are many opportunities for success as well as tremendous potential for frustration. One thing to keep in mind: Do not attack the media you want to work with at the first point of frustration. Your responsibility is to get positive coverage for your organization or cause. To do that you need to establish relationships. Getting good coverage is all about relationships and professional behavior, as you will see as you proceed through this book.

This does not mean that at some point you will not go public with criticism. In some cases, for a variety of reasons, the corporate media may clearly want to prevent your success. But the next time they might want to help. You have to be in a position to take advantage when they do.

Organizing against the media system is an important component for social change. But the organizing has to be smart and selective. It often helps if there are media watchdog groups who can take up your issue or other groups and individuals working on your issue who want to play a more provocative role with the media. Then it's possible to play "good cop/bad cop."

Agitation and bad publicity may move the media to be more responsive to you, but it might provoke a backlash. Attacking the media is tricky and must be thought through with people with whom you have trusting, working relationships, and there will be times when your values and commitment lead you to conclude the only way to live with yourself is to speak the truth in as powerful a way as possible. But remember, you may be burning bridges to the media.

Alternatives

Thousands of publications, some nonprofit, some for profit, present alternatives to corporate media. There are hundreds of community radio stations; many are affiliated with NPR and others with the more progressive Pacifica radio network, which has stations in New York, Los Angeles, Houston, Washington, D.C. and the Bay Area. There are hundreds of public TV stations across the land and many of them provide some local news and public affairs coverage. Add to that public access TV and the growing influence of Internet and Web-based media, and you can see there is a vast network of information sources.

The alternative media is diverse, comprehensive and situated in many media niches. The biggest weakness of the alternative media is its inability to reach larger audiences. In terms of print, the reason for this is obvious. Political and social content is not generally conducive to the selling of advertising. Magazines and newspapers cannot survive without advertising revenue or some other subsidy. In fact, the few noteworthy magazines of opinion do survive because of wealthy supporters who make contributions to make sure ideas are kept in discussion and stories do not disappear.

There are general-interest magazines of opinion like *The Nation*, *The Progressive* and *Mother Jones*. There are intellectual, women's, gay and lesbian, youth, people of color, community organizing and parenting magazines, and magazines for virtually every niche, all with a progressive orientation.

These small magazines have a long and proud history of keeping ideas alive, feeding networks of activists who work in coordination to push policy changes or raise public consciousness. At its best, alternative and independent media provide a lively contrast to the stories and commercialism that dominate mainstream media. Without the independent press, often one would not know that there are different ways of seeing things. Sometimes the alternative press will spot trends or break stories that eventually find their way to the corporate press.

Yet, one of the media's and advertising culture's most powerful weapons is co-optation and appropriation. Many radical images, hip concepts and tough investigative pieces are found in mainstream media, sometimes before they show up in the alternatives. One of the main reasons for this is

resources: Alternative media is often poorly funded and lacks promotional skill and marketing resources. Thus staff can be low-paid and inexperienced. The alternative press may also be wary of cooperating with social issues groups because they do not want to be pegged as supporters of progressive causes and not doing "good journalism."

Weekly newspapers

Besides PBS and NPR, the most widely known arenas of the alternative media are alternative weekly newspapers. The more than 150 of these papers in cities and university communities across the country reach millions of people. These papers are very uneven: some do very good work while others can be hostile to grassroots groups trying to get out their messages. Many of these papers have made lots of money and have become fairly well-establishment as well.

Consolidation has come to the alternative press, too. As this book is being prepared, two companies—The New Times group and Stern publications (owners of the *Village Voice*)—now each own approximately 10 papers in cities across the country, having bought out papers in Seattle, Minneapolis, Cleveland, St. Louis, San Francisco, Dallas, Houston and other localities. Sometimes the new owners invest more money in their papers, hire new writers and make their papers better. But sometimes the attitudes of people running these papers can be as arrogant or difficult to penetrate as the dailies.

Getting your point of view across takes a lot of effort but with careful planning can be extremely rewarding. Alternative and independent media outlets are important sources to include in your efforts.

1. The basics

Example
Soundbite

1 "They say Wall Street is whizzing, that stocks are up and the economy is good. It's whizzing all right, on you and me and other Americans that are working harder than ever for less and less." *(Jim Hightower, Radio commentator)*

2 "You don't have to be straight to be in the military, you just have to shoot straight." *(The late Governor Barry Goldwater, speaking in support of ending the ban on gays and lesbians serving in the armed forces)*

3 "The women of Idaho are not getting the health coverage they need to take care of themselves and their families because of unfair insurance practices. We need a prescription for fairness that covers all Idahoans and keeps our medicine cabinets stocked." *(Idaho Women's Network)*

4 "We want to be shareholders not sharecroppers." *(Rev. Jesse Jackson, launching a new campaign to place minorities in positions of power in corporations)*

Example
Framing

How is welfare reform framed? Is this a story about people who are not working and taking advantage of the hard efforts of working taxpayers, or is it about how every person living in this country deserves a decent wage as well as society's support? Gay and lesbian rights is another good example: One side has framed it as "special rights for homosexuals who choose to be gay and can be cured and made straight." The other side has framed it as an issue of equality, fairness and the need to end discrimination against gay people.

Media jargon

Soundbite

A "soundbite" is a short, pithy, attention-getting quote that communicates the gist of your message. Most TV and radio broadcast "bites" last 8 to 10 seconds. In print, you will probably get one quote that fills up one short paragraph, maybe two if you are lucky. The best bites contain action words, puns or verbal twists—even a touch of humor. Do not attempt to explain everything in your bite; that is a sound *banquet* that will be edited down to just one quick quote.

Spin

"Spin" is the art of influencing the outcome of a story. It is how you nudge, cajole, massage and direct the news. It is your angle on the story. Every side of a debate has its own spin. The White House, Congress, Pentagon and most major corporate and political institutions employ armies of "spinners" who do nothing but try to influence reporters. Media activists spin stories by working with reporters and "framing" the story to emphasize particular angles while downplaying others. Reporters like to consider themselves impervious to spin.

Counterspin

Every side of an argument will have its own spin; sometimes, therefore, we must "counterspin" our opposition. For example, opponents of San Francisco's Critical Mass bike rally—when bicyclists gather in downtown San Francisco the last Friday of every month to bike in solidarity—spun the issue as "irresponsible bike anarchists" unlawfully taking over the streets of downtown San Francisco. The San Francisco Bicycle Coalition **counterspun** it as an issue of "alternative transportation" that affects every resident of the city, especially those who do not own cars. Ultimately, the Bicycle Coalition won. Be prepared to spin your messages and counterspin those of your opponent (*see "A Case study: Media meltdown," page 96*).

Pitch

To "pitch" a story means to give an idea for a news story to reporters, producers or editors—and getting them excited about covering it. Activists pitch stories by calling up reporters, meeting with them in person or sending a story idea tip sheet. You must be enthusiastic about the idea and offer real news with additional sources.

Frame

The "frame" of the story is its boundaries, its borders, its defining limits, its impact and its significance. How you frame your news will determine not only whether a reporter covers it, but also whether your position is communicated effectively. Framing determines who is in the story and who is not; who are the good guys and who are the bad guys; who gets to define the issue and who gets to respond.

Framing is key. Whoever helps the reporter frame the story in a bigger, more significant way, gets the most press coverage—and the best. In much of mainstream media today, the story's frame is set by government, corporate and other "official" spokespeople. Getting into the frame—or changing the frame of the story altogether—is one of the greatest challenges.

Hook

A "hook" is a way to make the story more interesting to a reporter. Hooks are the components of a news story that make it irresistible to journalists: timeliness, anniversaries, controversy, localizing a national story and dramatic human interest. Think of your news as bait that is luring the fish to bite. Put the hook out there!

Hooks become part of your "frame." They give the story more impact and prominence (*see "Framing for our lives!," page 24*). You can hook your news to something else happening in the media, say a visit by a major politician or the president. Your hook could be a milestone: The 20th anniversary of Three Mile Island as a news story about ongoing community toxic pollution. Your hook could also be the release of a new report. Hooks can be "first ever" stories. Is what you are doing "unprecedented" or "groundbreaking"? If so, that is your hook.

Lead

In modern American news style, the "lead" is the first line or paragraph of a story; it represents the initial and central point. For example: "House Democrats today passed three amendments designed to block the full impact of Republican budget cuts on elderly Americans." Or: "Anti-war activists chained to paper and cardboard replicas of Polaris missiles blocked entrance to the Pentagon for five hours yesterday, in protest of continued U.S. deployment of nuclear arms in Saudi Arabia." In preparing your materials, anticipate the lead of a reporter's story—and help to provide it. In your own press releases and media advisories, try to write concise leads that will grab a reporter's attention. If you do not grab them by the end of the paragraph—or sometimes by the headline—they probably will not continue.

Op ed (opinion editorial)

Often written from a personal angle, "op eds" appear on the editorial page of newspapers or during the "point/counterpoint" portion of radio and TV shows. Writers pitch their op eds to the editorial editors. Op eds are useful to communicate points on an issue in your own words. They should be short, personal, and clearly state the key messages.

Photo op (photo opportunity)

Use "photo ops" to stage high-impact images that communicate your messages. Photographs and strong television pictures can move an audience much more directly than words. ACT UP, the national AIDS direct-action group, mastered the photo op in the mid-1980's as it protested government inaction in fighting the spread of HIV. Who can forget the powerful pictures of people living with AIDS sprawled in front of fake tombstones printed

---

Example
Hooks

August 1998 was the anniversary of the implementation of the welfare reform law signed in Washington by President Clinton. Across the country, local groups working on this issue hooked their local news to the anniversary and moved a message about how the reform was not working for everyone in their towns. The activists pitched the "two years later" milestone angle on the story and provided an update and local analysis.

Mother's Day comes around every year. Instead of the typical news story on Mother's Day—the new shopping mall is popular with moms—pitch the press an original story that hooks to the calendar holiday: a piece on welfare mothers trying to get child care; lesbian mothers raising kids in non-traditional families; or mothers with AIDS fighting against the disease.

with such slogans as "Killed By Government Bureaucracy?" Of course, the White House Communications Office also mastered the photo op during this time, staging such images as Ronald Reagan chopping wood on his ranch, driving his jeep and speaking at the Berlin Wall.

Wire service

"Wire services" are news sources that file articles to newspapers and radio and TV stations across the country; media outlets then "pull" the stories off the wire to print or air them locally. The Associated Press (AP) is probably the most popular wire service, with bureaus in most media markets. Other mainstream wire services include: Copley, Dow Jones, Gannett, Knight-Ridder, New York Times News Service, Reuters, Scripps-Howard, States and United Press International. Every media activist should have the number of the nearest AP bureau and other wire service offices in their rolodex. If you get a local story onto the AP wire, it can be picked up in papers nationwide.

Related news sources are **syndicated columnists**. These journalists write features that are syndicated—disseminated—to subscriber media outlets across the country.

Daybook

The "daybook" is the daily listing of events for journalists, including press conferences, rallies and other media events. It is often what reporters check first thing in the morning to see what news is being made that day. The AP produces one of the most popular daybooks. To get on the AP daybook, call or fax your local AP bureau with a media advisory.

B-Roll

These are the images shown on the screen as a television news anchor provides a voice-over for a story. "B-roll" is filmed throughout the day by crews, or can be taken from the station's file footage to illustrate frequently covered issues such as highway congestion, schools and education or drug abuse. Video provided by industry and interest groups can also be used as b-roll material.

Video News Release (VNR)

The video version of a press release or radio actuality, a VNR is a television news story that an organization produces using their own information, materials and spokespeople. A VNR generally includes on-camera quotes from key spokespeople and plenty of footage that illustrates the issue. The best VNRs do not look like self-promotion pieces for the organization, but instead actually resemble television news stories. VNRs have gotten a bad rap for good reasons lately as more and more corporations promote their products and services in the guise of news stories. VNRs are distributed (often via satellite) to news stations across the country. They can be extremely expensive to produce or they can be economically produced depending on the scope of the piece. News stations sometimes use pieces of the package, airing a few seconds of footage with their own anchors reading the news.

PSA (Public Service Announcement)

A "PSA" is a short—usually 15- to 30-second, sometimes one minute—free spot on radio or TV that announces an event or cause.

Actuality

An "actuality" is a news piece created for radio. Activists can produce their own radio actualities and send them to radio stations across the state. An actuality sounds just like it was produced by a radio reporter, containing quotes, sound effects and background noise. Relatively inexpensive to make, actualities are an important media tool that is often underused. (See *"News Radio," page 77.*)

"No comment"

"No comment" is a dangerous thing to say to a reporter. Rarely—if ever—use this phrase with a journalist. Saying "no comment" suggests one of two things: (1) You are hiding something; (2) You are so uninformed and caught by surprise that you are incompetent. If you absolutely cannot speak on an issue, respond with something such as: "Our lawyers have informed us that we cannot speak on that issue. However, what I can say is that we are here to serve the community in the most effective and committed way possible." Better yet, turn the question around so you can respond with a key message.

On/Off the record

Many people use these terms without knowing their technical implications. Contributing to the confusion is the fact that "on" and "off the record" mean different things to different reporters. Generally, you must presume that everything you say to a reporter at all times—including social and casual settings—is on the record. That means it is information that can be used with specific attribution—your name. For some journalists, off the record means the information can still be used, but without attribution. Sometimes sources will go off the record to impart sensitive information with which they do not want to be associated. For example, stories will often cite, "A White House official who asked not to be identified..." This means the person went off the record and the attribution is general—not specific by name. Going off the record first requires permission from the journalist. The journalist must agree to the terms. You must remember to go back on the record when it is appropriate. Once you say something, it cannot be reversed and made off the record.

A related distinction is "**deep background**." Deep background usually means that the information and your name cannot be used: Think "Deep Throat" and the Watergate scandal. On the whole, it is preferable to stay "on the record," but in certain circumstances "off the record" and "deep background" can be strategically useful.

Embargo

You can "embargo" your news for a specific date and time. This means reporters cannot publish or air the news until the stated embargo time. Embargoes are a way for you to get information into the hands of key journalists prior to an event. That way they can do a good job covering your news without ruining the "big surprise." For example, reports given to journalists in advance may be embargoed until the time and date of a press conference. The embargoed copies allow reporters to study your work and begin to prepare the story. You must write "EMBARGOED UNTIL *[Date]* AND *[Time]*" across all documents given to reporters in advance. Most responsible reporters do not break embargoes. Nevertheless, they are a risk.

Note: Beware of time differences! If your news is national or regional, remember to take time zones into account. An embargo of "noon" comes much earlier to New York than to Los Angeles.

Media "dos & don'ts"

Never lie to a reporter

Never lie to or intentionally mislead reporters. Why? Because they are going to find out sooner or later. And when they find out, your credibility is forever ruined. Trust and integrity are critical in your relationships with reporters. Strong relationships can mean fair and balanced coverage of your issues. Lie to a reporter and your integrity is destroyed. Lying is unethical and bad karma. Besides, isn't this about telling the *truth* about our issues?

Respect reporters' professionalism

Journalists are extremely proud and protective of their professionalism. It pays for you to respect that. After all, don't you like to be treated professionally? Never create fake journalism awards conveniently presented at your event as a way to lure journalists to your news. Most reporters work for media outlets with strict guidelines on gifts. For example, one newspaper forbids anything more than $5 in value. Finally, reporters are human. They like to be told they did a fair and balanced job. And if they did not, they are open to constructive criticism.

Never wing it

If you do not know the answer to a reporter's question, do not make up something. You will most likely say something that is either "off message" or regrettable—or both. If a reporter asks you a question and you do not know the answer, say so and either introduce someone who does know, or find out the reporter's deadline and promise to get back with the answer by deadline. And make sure you do it.

Translate for real people

Many of us work for organizations that use all kinds of acronyms, jargon, leftist rhetoric, mission-statement talk and inside lingo. Do not use this language with reporters. Translate all terms into language reporters and audiences will understand. Take, for example, the phrase "economic justice." Translate it into terms that mean something to people: The right to earn a decent paycheck so you can afford a quality education for your children, put food on the table and improve your life.

Speak in soundbites

Condense your message down to 10 seconds or less for radio and television. Do not try to explain everything in your soundbite. Obviously, take the time to educate reporters about the nuances and details of an issue. But when the tape is rolling, speak in soundbites.

Return reporters' phone calls

Make sure you take reporters' phone calls. If you regularly miss their calls, they will stop calling. Even if you do not know the answer to a question, be a resource. Tell a reporter: "You know, that's not my turf; but here are three people who do work on that. You should call them. Here are their numbers." Reporters will appreciate the help.

Similarly, if a message from a reporter is waiting for you, do not pick that time for a coffee break. Return the call immediately or get someone else to call.

Meet reporters' deadlines

Find out about reporters' deadlines: They live by them. The newspaper has to go to the printer. The TV show has to air. These are not flexible

---

The Brother-in-law test

To test if your message passes muster with regular folks, conduct what I call the useful "brother-in-law test." Pick a relative, friend or acquaintance who is not associated with your cause or organization, and see if they understand the issue. My brother-in-law is a decent, working-class, college-educated man who is involved in his suburban community. Occasionally I have tested messages and language out on him, sometimes with interesting results. Once I was doing media for an organization fighting "environmental racism." I bounced that term, which we contemplated using in our messages, off my brother-in-law. "Environmental racism...," he pondered. After a few moments he said, "Does that mean trees are prejudiced?" We scratched the term from the message.

—Robert Bray

times. If you have not called back by 3 or 4 p.m. at print newspapers, the reporter will get very nervous. By 4:30 p.m. you are out of the story. The same holds for TV news a couple of hours before air time.

If something big is happening in the news, make yourself available at deadline time and you may get into the story. For example, one organization that works on the rights of welfare recipients was in the office when President Clinton signed the welfare law in Washington. They released a statement, took calls, and were quoted in numerous articles. Be there. You may get only one shot. When something hot is going on, make sure you are in touch and know what is happening. Check your voice mail regularly.

One last point about deadlines: If a reporter sympathetic to your issue calls on deadline for a quote and you do not know what is going on, ask them to explain. Reporters may describe the news for you, knowing that it will help you make a comment. They are not necessarily putting words in your mouth, although sometimes it is easy to tell what kind of quote they want. Usually, the article is more or less done and your quote will serve to round it out. This is an excellent opportunity to make sure your point of view is included. Listen carefully. Think quickly. And stay on your message.

Appear more reasonable than your opponents

Whoever appears more reasonable is ahead of the game. This does not mean you can never be angry or sometimes even outraged. But be extremely conscious of using words that are sensationalistic or that portray your opponents as something they are not.

Stake out your ground in positive terms and check the extreme language. Say what you stand for and how it will improve your communities, all the while putting your opponents on the defense. Be careful about labeling them. It may feel cathartic to call the bad guy a "nazi fascist," but that language will probably alienate people and certainly does not communicate a strategic message. We can express anger in the press, but channel and convert that rage into a message that moves people to awareness and action on your issues.

Remember: "three" is a trend

Three is a trend in the media—or so goes the old axiom. And trends are news. That means if you can find three examples of something—three single welfare mothers who are doing something to overcome their hardship, three examples of discrimination, three points of view that are similar on a particular story—you will position the story for better coverage. These examples reflect a "growing lead."

If it bleeds it leads

This is especially true about TV. Though it may reflect the sad state of American media, this is the reality. The point is drama sells. A news editor has to make choices: Run the piece on the horrible 16-car pile-up on the local freeway more prominently, using dramatic footage of rescuers prying people out of the cars and rushing them to the emergency room, or run the boring press conference in a fluorescent lit room with people in suits talking about some obscure policy. Which would *you* rather watch?

Stage and package your news for maximum media impact. Do not spill blood, but include dramatic human-interest stories, poignant anecdotes as well as compelling individuals and their testimonials. Obviously, the 16-car pile-up was not "staged." But to compete with the daily news, you have to present *your* news so it contains some human drama. Pick a setting that visually demonstrates the content of your message. If it is a children's issue, hold your event at a childcare center, playground or school; if it is environmental, choose a lakeside or toxic waste dump—though make sure it is not too far out of the way for the media to cover it. Make your event as appealing, personal and dramatic as possible. But do not go overboard. Be real. It is OK to be emotional; your internal alarms will start to sound if you are going overboard in the drama department.

Visualize your story for TV

Television is a visual medium. For every eight or 12 seconds of "soundbites" you may get into a TV news story, there will be another 30 to 45 seconds of visual material shown in the background. When planning your event, think how your message can be conveyed visually as well as verbally. If you have a short piece of video that illustrates your message, by all means give it to the reporter for use as "b-roll." (Greenpeace used to do this to great effect on their anti-whaling campaigns.) And do not forget to stage photo ops for print media as well.

Personalize your story

As much as possible, personalize your story to the media. If the issue is welfare reform and you are personally affected by it, say so: "As a welfare mother…" or "As a former welfare mother…" Other examples include: "As a teacher…" "As a father of three kids…" "As the daughter of an immigrant…" or "As someone who grew up in the Depression…" Reporters find this irresistible. Find individuals who personally represent the story. In the PR business, these people are often called "poster children." As tacky as that may seem, it works.

Think strategically

Think in terms of how media coverage affects your goals. As a community leader or someone responsible for an issue or organization, you are not seeking media coverage just to get your name in the newspaper. You are doing it because you have been entrusted by people in your community to have a leadership role and to achieve certain goals. Speaking to the press has implications not just for you and your organization, but for people around you. Do not just say, "Hey look, I got my name in the paper!" You have to think strategically about what you are saying and the impact it will have. How does it advance your issue? Your program? Your organization? How will it help you reach your goals? Think carefully about what you are saying—and why.

Do not answer reporters' questions, respond to them

If you learn nothing else from this guidebook, understand this last point: Every time you speak to a reporter—on the phone, at a rally with a camera in your face or to a reporter at a press conference—consider the interaction as an opportunity to move your message. Do not answer with what you think the reporter wants you to say, or what your opponents are saying. Respond with *your* messages (*see "Key Media Messages," page 26*).

Obviously, you have to answer some questions a reporter asks you: your name, age and affiliation, for example. But even this can be an opportunity to communicate your broader message. For example, when one activist was asked her age she responded: "I'm 42 years old; but like many people in their 40s, I am concerned about this issue because…" This activist not only answered the reporter's question, but also used the occasion to *respond* and advance a strategic message.

Example
Responding, not answering

When I worked in the gay rights movement, one of the most frequently asked questions by reporters was "How many homosexuals are there in America?" Typically I thought: "How the hell do I know? I know there's Bill in Seattle; there's Susan in Atlanta; there's Ellen in Hollywood…" My next impulse was to give some really boring and technical answer such as: "The Kinsey Institute, America's preeminent sexuality research specialists, reports that the number of homosexuals my be 10 percent of the population if you count same-sex tendencies from adolescence through adulthood. However, that figure was challenged by a University of Chicago study that said only six percent… blah, blah, blah."

Finally, I simply responded to the question with my own message, regardless of what the reporter might have wanted to hear. "No one really knows how many gay and lesbian people there are because we are an invisible minority. But we are found in every community. The real issue is that not one of us should ever be discriminated against or be the victim of violence."

I did not answer the question; I responded with my message about discrimination and violence. This strategy is extremely important to use when working with the press. Respond with your key messages and repeat them over and over—no matter what the question. This is your spin.

—Robert Bray

Six steps to success

The following is a six-step process for making news. Every organization or individual seeking media attention should follow this process in the order presented to maximize their media potential. What is the secret to scoring good press that will create change for your community? Read on.

1 Establish your goals

Before embarking on a media campaign, clearly articulate your desired goals. The goals drive press efforts—not the other way around. Everything you do in the media is designed to help you attain your goals. The goals should also be realistic.

Typical goals might be:
- Pass bill XYZ.
- Kill ordinance 123.
- Secure endorsements by select opinion and political leaders.
- Educate public about the issue.
- Stop discriminatory practices.
- Enhance the profile and visibility of your organization.
- Change misconceptions about an issue.
- Give voice to unheard people affected by the issue.

2 Identify your news

Do not waste reporters' time with something that is not news. What reports, surveys or briefing papers can you produce and release that will provide a new perspective? What media events that communicate real news can you stage? What information can you provide that will present a different twist to the story?

3 Target your audience

Identify the people who need to hear your message and who must be moved to action so your goals will be attained.

4 Frame the issue for maximum media impact

Do you always find yourself on the defense, with your opposition framing the news instead of you framing it? The news is not just about your group or your report. It is about something much bigger, with more drama, which will impact more people at a timely moment.

5 Craft your strategic media messages

Condense your complicated issue down to two or three main messages. Discipline the messages.

6 Create a media plan

Your plan will have several components, including everything from identifying and pitching reporters, to placing op eds, to staging media events. A coordinated media plan will increase your success in moving your messages and having them "echoed" through the media (see "Checklist for planning your media," page 38).

Targeting your audience

Any public relations effort must target your audience. This is one of the first tasks you must tackle in order to make news. Who are you trying to reach? You may have several target audiences who need to receive your message, or you may have one specific audience. The targeted audience will help determine the scope of your media plan. Give your audience some thought before embarking on a media campaign. This is good strategic planning.

Define your audience(s)

The target group for your message may include:
- Lawmakers
- Voters
- Opinion-makers
- Community leaders
- People of color
- People of faith
- Women
- Youth
- Gays, lesbians, bisexuals and transgenders
- College students
- Retirees
- Others

Plan your media for your desired audience

Why waste resources on a media plan that will not reach your targeted audience? If home mechanics are a target audience, pitch your story to the "Home" section of the local newspaper or to the "handy home tips" local radio show. If local residents are important, aim for the "Metro" section of the paper and community press, including ethnic media that may serve affected neighborhoods. Aiming for local politicians? Then stage a media event on the steps of City Hall or your state capitol.

Match your media and organizing plans to reach targeted audiences

Door-to-door flyering, a local community "speak out" or other education efforts can be timed to coincide with the placing of an opinion editorial in the local paper, or the staging of a local media event.

By targeting your audience and appropriate media you will maximize your resources and create a more effective media plan.

Example
Defining your audience

Imagine you are releasing a new report on the impact of petroleum-based waste dumping in your community. The report contains useful information for residents who unknowingly contribute to the waste—by pouring car oil down the drain—plus exposes how government inaction has allowed industrial polluters to spew harmful chemicals by the tons into the local well water supply. This situation affects the entire city, but disproportionately affects low-income people living near the big refineries. You want the report to spark community outrage, educate the public about what they can do to help and pressure your city council to take action. Target audiences might include: residents who change the oil in their cars, including home mechanic types and do-it-yourself grease monkeys; low-income people and people of color who must endure the refinery waste; local and state elected officials who have the power to force the refineries to stop polluting; and columnists and talk show hosts who care about the issue.

All of your target audiences will get their news from outlets relevant to their lives. Those media outlets should then be targeted. For example, home mechanics may read the "Fix it Yourself" section in the local paper.

2. The message, the frame

Framing the news

"Far from being an objective list of facts, a news story results from multiple subjective decisions about whether and how to present happenings to media audiences. Newsmakers engage in a selection process, actively making sense out of an immense quantity of experience, selecting some points as critical, discarding or downplaying others." —Charlotte Ryan, *Prime Time Activism*

Understanding framing is one of the most important steps to understanding how the media can work for you—or against you. The frame of the story is its boundaries, its borders, its defining limits, its impact. How you frame a story is critical. Whoever helps the reporter frame the story in a more significant manner gets the most press coverage—and the best.

Who is in the story and who is not? Who are the good guys and who are the bad guys? Who gets to define the issue and who gets to respond? All are determined by your frame.

Government officials, corporate heads, interest groups and think tanks all employ public relations experts whose sole job is to get their point of view in the media. In other words, to help set the frame. Editors and reporters must make choices every day about what stories make the news and whose point of view is going to be in the story. How you frame the story will help determine whether or not you are included in the news.

Take the example of welfare.

The official frame on welfare is something like this: This country was founded on individualism. Every individual—not our society—needs to pick himself up and take care of himself. No more welfare cheats.

The reproduction of images of people who do drugs, refuse to work or are welfare cheats, all work to reaffirm the frame's legitimacy. At the same time, the frame absolves government of the responsibility to take care of its citizens.

To get yourself in the frame—or change the frame altogether—you have to think strategically. What is the issue? What is your objective? What is your goal? What are you trying to accomplish both politically and socially?

Returning to the welfare example: Are you trying to get people off welfare and into decent jobs? Are you trying to empower people who are on welfare? Are you trying to pass or defeat specific legislation that is moving through the legislature? Define your goal and attach it to the frame.

Next, think about what symbols carry the frame. The "official" frame will try to squeeze in an unemployed black mother with 15 kids. You have to counter that with whoever represents your point

Framing Example
Rats bite baby

Charlotte Ryan, noted national media critic and advocate, cites an example of framing in her book, *Prime Time Activism* (South End Press, 1991). It involves a newspaper headline and story concerning an event, or series of events, in an American inner-city. Whether it is hypothetical or real does not matter. This example should help you understand the whole subject of framing.

Imagine this headline in the metro section of a major urban daily: "Rats bite baby."

The story is set in a housing project in the black inner-city community of a large metropolis. It involves a single mother who left her baby in the crib while she went down to the corner to cash her welfare check. The door was left open so her neighbors could hear. While she was gone, the baby was bitten repeatedly by rats. A neighbor responded to the cries of the infant and brought the child to Central Hospital where he was treated and released in his mother's custody.

How is this story being framed? Who are the bad guys? Not the rats. Not the city. Not the owner of this project. It is the mother who left her baby alone to go and cash her welfare check. The bad guys here are all welfare recipients and unwed mothers—especially people of color. The good guys are upstanding citizens who work or get off welfare, as well as politicians who advocate welfare reform. The images that communicate this frame are the photos of people hanging around the local check cashing business, abandoned children playing in the project and politicians calling for welfare reform. Now let's look at another variation:

"Rats bite infant: Landlord, tenants dispute blame"

Suddenly, the frame has changed considerably. Now it is a *60 Minutes*-style story: the slumlord hounded by cameras in his wealthy neighborhood, his jacket over his head, jumping into his Mercedes and driving away surrounded by a phalanx of lawyers. This version of the story includes information from other tenants who claim that their repeated requests for rodent extermination had been ignored by the landlord. An image that communicates this of view: The single mom struggling to make it against a system of vast injustice and indifference with no job training; the children caught in the middle. You have to change the frame of the story by changing as many of its components as possible: the characters, the goals, the terms of debate.

When asked to describe how our opponents frame welfare, we usually respond quickly because it is easy to see how they are doing it. But when asked how *we* frame the subject, anti-poverty activists often go off in many different directions. We need to step back from our work and contemplate how we are framing our issues and what messages we are communicating.

Whoever frames the issue in the broadest way—so it affects the most people—will, in the competitive media market, get the coverage.

Unfortunately, many activists have not taken the time to frame their issues and simply react to the frame of their opposition. Give yourself the space to really analyze the issue, construct the news for your benefit and put your opponents on the defense.

The power of framing

- How you frame your news will determine its prominence in the media.
- How you frame your news will determine the competitiveness of your story as compared to all the other news happening that day.
- How you frame your news will define the debate.
- How you frame your news will define the players: Who are the good guys and who are the bad guys.
- How you frame your news will persuade people to respond in a particular way, including public officials, voters and regular community members.
- How you frame your news will inform the public about your position and will communicate your messages.
- How you frame your news will determine what images and metaphors communicate the story.

23

frame is one of angry and concerned residents of the project coming together to protest. Though the landlord tries to blame the tenants for improperly disposing of their garbage, the frame has been expanded. The facts will now be selected and ordered differently, guided by a different set of values and responsibilities. Still something is missing. Consider this:

"Rat bites rising in city's 'Zone of Death'"

The frame has changed again. Now City Hall is implicated: Elected officials, urban policy, economic empowerment zones and affordable housing become part of the story. The whole inner-city context is under fire. According to this version of the story, the woman's baby is only the latest victim of a "rat epidemic" plaguing inner-city neighborhoods in the "Zone of Death." The good guys and the bad guys have changed places. The mother, vilified in the first "Rats bite baby" story, has now become a spokesperson for families victimized in the urban "Zone of Death." She becomes the emblem of the story. The frame of the story—its focus, its boundaries, its underlying values—has

changed. Meanwhile, the story has moved from page 5C to page 1A of the local paper and is the lead TV story.

This is what you must do for your news. You can set the frame. You can create the messages, the images and the significance of the story in a way that puts you on the offense. You can shape public opinion by strategically framing the story and communicating messages. This is the most empowering thing you can do as you communicate with the media.

When you go to the press with your message, you help to change the terms of debate. Among all the technical ways you can begin to do that, the most important one is deciding what message you choose to communicate. The next section of this guidebook focuses on messages. Understand that you have a window of opportunity to seize; to do so, you first need a frame. With issues like welfare, economic opportunity, abortion, civil rights or human rights, we are framing for our lives. The better we are at doing it, the more we are going to be heard.

Framing for our lives!
Hang your frame on these news hooks

Every frame needs a hook. Hooks help you catch reporters' attention. Hooks make stories more newsworthy. They can be included in the framing of a story in a way that expands the significance of the news. When you pitch a story (*see "Pitching your story," page 52*) and frame the news for the reporter, consider including as many of these hooks as possible:

New announcement
Is your news "unprecedented," "groundbreaking" or "first ever?" If so, say it. The rule of the game is: Reporters are only interested in new news, not old news. Make your news fresh.

Trend
Reporters naturally are interested in trends. Stories that suggest new opinions, behavior patterns and attitudes might get covered. Trends can be revealed in "groundbreaking" reports that detail new information (*see "Making news with your report," page 66*). And remember: In the news business, "three is a trend." Find at least three examples to corroborate your assertion that a new trend is emerging.

Localize a national story
A convenient news hook is to take a nationally breaking story and emphasize its local impact. For example, when President Clinton signed the welfare reform bill, the local angle could have been framed to emphasize how this legislation would affect real people living in your town.

The other side of this framing hook is: **Nationalize a local story**. If your local news has state, regional or national implications, by all means include that in your frame. Similarly, if your news hooks to a nationally known symbol, include that in your frame. For example, activists in San Antonio battling a freedom of expression/censorship issue were encouraged to hook the frame to the Alamo. (Don't gag, it can work.) The story was pitched, "In the shadow of the Alamo, A modern day national battle rages over artistic sovereignty."

Dramatic human interest
Compelling personal stories almost *have* to be part of the frame. Flesh out the frame to include the stories of real people, their triumphs and tragedies, ordeals, adventures and anecdotes. This is a talk show nation so spill a little drama in your news. Besides, the stories are true and represent the voices of people who are often not included.

Controversy
This sells stories, for good or for bad. Your opposition is obviously framing the story to downplay the controversy or emphasize their agenda: "It's about jobs, not spotted owls!" says the anti-environment timber industry. So you should frame the controversy to put your opponent on the defense. Besides, there

---

Points to remember when framing your news:

Frame for maximum media impact
Why is your story so important that it will compete with all the other news for a reporter's attention? You must frame the story to capture a reporter's interest. Frame so your news has the potential of appearing on Page 1A of your local newspaper.

Frame for widest reach and drama
This means you should think about: How many people will be affected; what the controversy is in terms of political or cultural policy and conflicts; and how wide is the reach of the story? Will your news only impact 29 people in your community, or does the issue have a much broader scope and ultimately will affect every person in your state? Aim high with your frame.

Define the issue and players
Whoever defines the debate controls it. Move your frame, not the frame of your opponents. The frame will determine who are the "good guys" and who are the "bad guys." Frame so the opposition is on the defense and forced to counterframe, and you are on the offense, having claimed the political and moral high ground.

Target your reporters and frame the story appropriately
How you frame for your local business reporter will be different than how you frame an issue for the lifestyle or political desks. How you would frame for *Oprah* is different from how you would frame for *The Wall Street Journal*. Customize your frame to fit the picture!

24

is hardly an issue we work on that is *not* controversial. Spotlight political conflicts, civic malfeasance, corporate greed, the will of the people being undermined, open betrayal of the public's trust, laws broken, opinions clashing or scandals erupting.

Fresh angle on an old story

Same as news being "new" (*see previous example: "New announcement"*). If you can take an old story and put a fresh twist on it, make that part of your frame. The age old example is: "Dog Bites Man," a non-story. "Man Bites Dog," now that is a story.

Anniversaries

One year later, one decade later, 20 years later. These "anniversary" stories are attention-grabbers. For example, the Center For Health, Environment and Justice launched a huge, multi-state media campaign around the 20th anniversary of the Love Canal toxic pollution debacle to communicate messages about toxic pollution in neighborhoods today. They scored volumes of media hits through their savvy playing of the anniversary hook (*see "Case study: PR Consultants at work," page 84*).

Calendar hook

Frame your story to capture something coming up on the calendar. "Back to school" can be a hook for toxic pollution in your children's schools. Mother's Day can be a hook for a new breast or cervical cancer community hot line. Earth Day can be a hook for environmental injustice in a local low-income neighborhood. Valentine's Day can be a hook for your domestic partnership or gay and lesbian marriage controversy.

Profiles and personnel

Your news may feature individuals, community leaders or galvanizing spokespersons who may become news themselves because of their fascinating stories.

Special event

If you are staging a huge conference, rally or gathering, frame the event to capture the issue and signify its importance.

Respond and react

Most of what we describe in this section is about proactively framing your news for maximum media impact. However, consider reacting to news made by others as an opportunity to counterframe the issue and move your messages. For example, when President Clinton signed the welfare bill, local organizations working with low-income people released statements counterframing the issue and exposing the troubling implications of the bill in their own communities. They used this hook to "jam" their own message in local coverage.

Celebrity

Sometimes fame and fortune can be part of the frame and serve as a hook. If you have a nationally known luminary—cultural, religious, political or entertainment—make sure he or she is included in the story. Celebrities attract the news. The downside to celebrity is, of course, it tends to outshine the stories of real people actually affected by the issue. Plus, celebrities are often famous simply for being famous, not necessarily for their political acumen or experience.

Example
Special event hook

The National Gay and Lesbian Task Force hosts an annual Creating Change Conference every November, the weekend after election day. The Conference, a grassroots organizing event that attracts thousands of lesbian, gay, bisexual and transgender community leaders from across the nation, is framed to represent the gathering of the gay movement right after Election Tuesday. Leading gay representatives analyze the elections, determine how gays voted and present the outcome of the elections and the impact on gay and lesbian Americans—all at the conference. This often lures the political press to the event and scores media hits for the conference itself.

Key media messages

After framing your issue, developing and "disciplining" your key messages is possibly the most important part of your media plan. All of your media efforts must be aimed at moving the message. Your spokespersons must be on message (see "*Being a better spokesperson*," *page* 33). The message must be echoed through different sources, such as press releases, media events, opinion editorials and letters to the editor. Messages will be targeted to different audiences.

We must be more proactive in articulating messages that resonate with our communities. Following are the key pointers you need to know about media messages.

Message essentials

Messages capture action, advocacy and political/cultural position. They help frame the issue.

What are you advocating? Which side of the argument do you support? Whose interests are at stake? Your messages communicate your frame, your position and your call for action.

Condense your issue into key messages

No matter how simple or complex your issue, the utmost discipline is required to distill what you want to say into concise messages. Remember, you do not have to cover every policy nuance or expound on social history in your messages. There will be room for details in your background materials. Your messages should capture the essence of the issue at hand in the most accessible way possible.

Repeat your messages—over and over

You will know you have mastered this rule when you cannot stand hearing yourself repeat your messages anymore. Advertisers know this trick well. That is why you see the same slogan everywhere. Sooner or later, the message will permeate your consciousness and you will buy the product—or at least know it is for sale. Politicians realize this too. They repeat their soundbites until they sink in and you have a sense of what they stand for—or say they do. Every talk you give to a community group, every interview you give to the press, every letter to the editor you write, every press release and PSA you issue, all must contain your key messages.

Respond to reporters' questions with key messages

Remember the cardinal rule of successful spin: Do not **answer** a reporter's questions, **respond** to them. Do not lie or misrepresent the truth; rather look at every question as another opportunity to communicate your messages regardless of what the reporter is asking.

Use messages to direct the interview

The audience is the target. The reporter is the conduit to disseminate your messages. However, the reporter may be familiar with a different frame on your issue, or be interested in exploring a tangential issue in more detail. Use your messages to anchor the interview and you will be better able to steer it in the direction you want.

Stay "on message"

Discipline the message. Do not get pulled off message. This is not as easy as it sounds. No matter how outrageous the opposition gets, remember to stay calm, keep your discipline and bring the focus back to your messages.

Many messengers, one message

In the PR business, when the same message is repeated by many different messengers from many different angles, it is called "echo." No one can get out a message alone. Today's media marketplace is so saturated with information that we need to work together just to be heard. When echo works, it is not just one person out there repeating the message. People see the same message in op eds and in letters to the editor, hear it in PSAs, and watch it on the evening news. And the beauty of it is, everyone is on message!

Message reminders

- **Do not answer reporters' questions, respond to them.**
- **Speak in soundbites.**
- **Repeat your messages.**
- **Stay "on message."**
- **Make "key messages" your mantra.**

Case study

Developing and moving key messages

Approaching the media may seem like a daunting task. Given the history of narrow and superficial coverage of important social issues by mainstream media, grassroots groups and community organizers often feel overwhelmed by the task of contacting reporters and getting them interested in a story.

However, with careful consideration and planning, a successful media campaign can impact the way Americans feel and think about an issue. Grabbing the media's attention–by locking in on an appropriate frame and developing key messages– will make this happen.

One group–Jobs with Justice (JWJ)–examined what was happening in the media with regards to welfare reform. On the national level, media coverage of economic fairness did not reflect the local realities. The national press' portrayals of recipients moving off the welfare rolls failed to investigate a crucial aspect of the welfare reform process: What job opportunities did ex-welfare recipients have? In its organizing efforts and research, JWJ found that the jobs were not there.

The following thoughts of Fred Azcarate, JWJ's executive director, and Simon Greer, JWJ's Workers' Rights Board project director, explain the importance of developing key messages and coordinating a national and local media campaign around these messages.
—Seeta Peña Gangadaharan

What is the issue?

Jobs with Justice is a national coalition of more than 60 labor, community and faith-based organizations with a 10-year history of fighting for workers' rights and economic justice. In the spring of 1997, during a national planning meeting, local leaders felt that the issue needing most attention was welfare reform and workfare. While a solid network of welfare organizations based in Washington, D.C. connected regularly with the national press corps to help shape public opinion on welfare/workfare issues, we felt the coverage did not reflect the reality of local issues. Media were touting the decrease in the numbers of welfare rolls without focusing on what was happening to people going off the rolls. There was no broad, coordinated mobilization of grassroots folks to get their own stories out into the media.

We were challenged to develop a key message based on local experiences that would help to reframe the debate and show where welfare reform was lacking both locally and nationally. We decided to create a National Day of Action, scheduled for Human Rights Day: December 10, 1997. We had six months to work with, giving our member groups considerable lead time to allow them to really make sense of what was happening locally.

Since we are Jobs with Justice, the jobs angle was the key hook for us. Our central, overarching message was "The jobs aren't there." Together with the Preamble Center for Public Policy, we commissioned two reports to be released in conjunction with our Day of Action. The first—using the stark testimonies of ten people in different cities across the country who were directly affected by new state welfare policies—aimed to show the personal side of welfare reform. The second—

a more statistical report—provided factual support from each state to clearly demonstrate how few jobs were actually available to current welfare recipients trying to meet federal workfare requirements.

Knowing our message beforehand—"The jobs aren't there"— helped us tremendously with the oversight of these reports. The Preamble Center worked with us for two months prior to the Day of Action. They loaned us one full-time staff person and one person at half time. Together, we put an enormous amount of energy into producing material. We wanted our reports and media events to reflect and directly bolster our key message.

Fred Azcarate
Executive Director
Jobs with Justice
501 Third Street, NW
Washington DC 20001
(P) 202 434-1106
(F) 202 434-1477
(E) jobswjustice@jwj.org
www.jwj.org

What works: getting everyone involved

With groups in 60 cities wanting to participate in this campaign, we had to face the challenge of coordinating our common message in each area. To do so, we approached the media plan from the following premise: We could get excellent coverage if the release of JWJ's reports from our national office coincided with Day of Action rallies that local chapters organized. There was both a national and a local relevance to our story that made it an attractive news hook.

Some time before the Day of Action, we did a national conference call with our local affiliates who were planning to approach their local media. We set up a few people on the line to discuss how welfare reform and workfare were typically framed by mainstream media, go over our strategy and hone our key message: "The jobs aren't there." After reviewing key messages, we express-

continued on next page

mailed our reports to everyone involved in the campaign.

We had nearly 70 endorsing organizations, including groups unaffiliated with our coalition, who helped us achieve our goals. The American Federation of State, County and Municipal Employees (AFSCME) taped radio actualities that they shopped around to many radio stations, eventually getting more than 150 radio spots. The AFL-CIO mailed reports to 150 media outlets, and the Service Employees International Union (SEIU) lent us a press person to do calls to media contacts. In fact, one of the SEIU press people conducted a search of those who had covered the job gap during the year, and then created an effective database of reporters for us to contact.

On the morning of December 10 we were surprised by a call from the White House. They wanted to respond to the claims made in our reports. A later story in the Associated Press about the JWJ campaign quoted both key spokespersons from JWJ and White House press secretary Mike McCurry! The position taken by the White House underscored the seriousness of welfare reform/workfare as a whole, not just the efforts of JWJ. We counted this as a major victory, especially considering a story on the AP wire meant we had influenced debate in places where we had not even planned an action.

What doesn't work: The challenges

Although we had a good message and professional-looking set of media deliverables, we could have taken better advantage of our position. For example, we did not get any coverage in *The Washington Post*—and we are located in D.C. We completely underplayed this outlet and thus missed an incredible opportunity to make news in one of the nation's most influential mainstream papers.

In retrospect, we should have conducted press briefings with *The Washington Post*. With our media kit and active staff in D.C., and in light of the coverage we were receiving nationwide, the *Post* could not have ignored a meeting where we sat down and discussed the context and timeliness of the Day of Action story.

Television was another of our weak spots. While many local coalitions got good TV coverage, we were not able to get much national coverage. Besides a short CNN piece, we were blacked out on national TV. We feel the reason for this is that we lacked photo opportunities. For example, we did a "musical chairs" skit in front of the U.S. Chamber of Commerce that National Public Radio (NPR) picked up and used for a sound clip in their report. The point was to illustrate what was said in our job gap report: People being kicked off the welfare rolls would be fighting and scrambling for too few well-paying jobs. However, there was no corresponding case with television. We should have paid closer attention to targeting TV.

Concluding thoughts

In view of our success, we feel that certain things worked particularly in our favor. First, we are in the fortunate position of being a national organization that is grounded locally. On the national level, we have a staff of three people. Our media plans were all carried out in-house by those three people in the D.C. office. Furthermore, our network of local affiliates gave us additional support; about half of our local offices raise money to build full-time staff. In total, we had about 15 people, spread throughout the country, helping us.

Since we are a member-based organization, it was important that we created roles for our members in our media strategy. We included endorsement statements from national organizations that supported the Day of Action in our press kit. Local folks who attended our steering committee meetings were approached by the national staff to officially endorse the action. By going through a formal process of endorsement, these liaisons became active agents, promoting the Day of Action within their own organizations.

Second, media was just a small piece of what we did. We had 60 actions around the country, all of which marched and rallied on December 10. The combination of having both hard facts and a human face to illustrate a story with both a national scope and significant local activity made it pretty irresistible for the media.

Finally, and obviously, it was not just our media planning alone that prompted our success. We also lucked out in terms of timing. Media coverage in 1997 was all about how welfare was working. Toward the end the year, something changed. All of a sudden the question became: "Where are the people who are moving off welfare going?" This new angle, combined with the fact that states' proposals for welfare reform were due the same week as our Day of Action, caused reporters to tune in and take note. Our message was clear: You can try anything you want, but "There aren't any jobs." The tide was turning and we rode the wave.
　　　　　　　　　　　　　　　—Fred Azcarate

A model for your messages
Problem, solution and action

Your key messages should communicate in a succinct and pithy way the most critical components of your issue. Do not try to explain everything; instead, condense your issue down to two or three strategic messages.

Try this model for creating and sharpening your key messages. Condense your issue into three media messages: 1) The Problem; 2) The Solution; and 3) The Call to Action. Literally write out a couple of sentences per message onto a "message talking points" page. The following example is from the "Job Gap and Welfare Reform" Day of Action, organized by Jobs with Justice in December 1997. These messages were communicated to scores of community activists nationwide, who then held media events to move the messages locally.

Message 1. **The problem**

What is the problem you are working to address? Again, forget the mountains of minutiae you have gathered on your issue. Step back and look at the big picture. Take a moment to create a message that *frames* the problem clearly, broadly and in as compelling a way as possible. Whoever frames the problem controls the terms of the debate. Message #1 is the framing message. It will communicate the scope of the issue or problem and dramatize its impact.

Message 2. **The solution**

While defining the problem is crucial, if you just stop there you will be in danger of sounding like a whiner. Be sure to move on to the next message: the solution. Message #2 is the "values" message. Use it to communicate a sense of your values: In what kind of society do you want to live? How do you want people to be treated? What do you stand for? Make sure to provide hope in your solution message.

Message 3. **A call to action**

You have already defined the problem and offered a solution. Now, what do we need to do to get to the solution? That is the call to action. The action call may be different depending on your targeted audience. What you ask the governor, state legislature and elected officials to do might be different from what you ask regular voters or community members to do.

Now that you have a model for preparing your key messages, practice delivering them—from Message No. 1 right through Message No. 3. The messages must move together: "The problem is X, but the solution is Y. That is why we are calling on the state legislature to pass Z."

Are the messages soundbites?

Yes and no. Consider using this three message model as an aid to help you cut through the complexities of your issue and focus on the key points. This will also help you frame the issue.

Sometimes, you will not have the time to communicate all three, but only enough time—say ten seconds—to make your case. Still, go through all your messages, and the chances of one "hitting" will be greater.

Message 1 Example

Welfare reform is failing in many places, not because welfare recipients do not want to work, but because not enough living wage jobs are available. *The jobs are not there.* This "job gap" has caused thousands of people to toil in horrible working conditions, without health and safety precautions and for sub-minimum wages. This has disastrous consequences for families and all taxpayers.

Message 2 Example

To make welfare reform work requires the creation of living wage jobs—decent paying jobs with health and safety for workers. The economic security and human dignity of American workers and low-income families depend on it.

Message 3 Example

Join our Day of Action to make sure that all workers of our state have decent living wages. The deadline for states to submit their spending proposals for federal welfare-to-work funds is this month. We want to send a clear message to our state officials: Close the job gap. Help us signal a new national call for jobs with justice and reform with dignity.

Visionary vocabulary Key words to convey values in your messages

"The difference between the almost right word and the right word is a large matter—it's the difference between the lightening bug and the lightening."
— Mark Twain

The way you talk about your issues can make all the difference in the world. If you want your message to have the impact of a lightening strike—and not the brief flash of a lightening bug—then vision and values are a crucial part of what you have to say. To help people understand your issue, you must first broaden your message and use language that will connect with the largest number of people.

As you craft your message, it is important to use simple, specific, easy-to-understand language. No tech talk or insider jargon! Talk about your issues in a way that all people can personally relate to by linking your messages to the core values that we all care about—family, health, safety, security, respect, fairness. Help your audience understand what is at stake for them.

Use hard-hitting action words that will grip your audience by the heart or hit them right in the gut. These words are the antidote to stifling jargon and "bureaucrat-ese" that deadens much political discourse. For example, instead of saying "The factory runoff will negatively impact the surrounding residents," say "The toxic poison will imperil the lives of hard-working people and endanger their community."

Words such as compassion, fairness, heritage, justice, etc. all connect with people's core values. Use these and other hard-hitting action words to flesh out your messages. What words can you add to this list?
—Holly Minch

Activate	Dignity	Injure	Relief
Advocate	Diversity	Integrity	Respect
Affirm	Endanger	Jeopardize	Responsible
American	Energize	Justice	Risk
Assist	Engage	Legacy	Safeguard
Balance	Equality	Mobilize	Strengthen
Bedrock	Fairness	Nation	Support
Benefit	Faith	Neighborhood	Sustain
Bold	Family	Nourish	Threaten
Champion	Fighting	Nurture	Tolerance
Change	Forward	People	Tradition
Community	Harm	Power	Trust
Compassion	Health	Preserve	Unity
Confirm	Help	Pride	Value
Damage	Heritage	Principle	Working
Defend	Honor	Progress	
Degrade	Hope	Promote	
Democracy	Hurt	Protect	
Destroy	Imperil	Public	

My progressive values

Personally, I would say that economic justice, a clean and healthy environment, equality for all and basic compassion and respect for human dignity are just a few progressive values that I hold dear. In crafting my messages, I would consider which of these and other values is most relevant and think about how to communicate that value effectively. It is not beneficial to talk in only technical terms about your issue: "The 1.3 million people on welfare" or "the 69 parts per million of methyl bromide in the local ground water." I believe we should have our values at the core of our messages. Our opponents certainly focus on *their* values: Down-sized government, family values, immigration reform, welfare cheats and big business incentives—to name a few. What are *our* values? We need to step back from our day-to-day reality as community activists and think about our power to communicate a vision that is based on equality, fairness and compassion. That, in many ways, is a major part of the solution message.
–Robert Bray

Focus groups and polls

Seeta Peña Gangadharan

Focus groups are one helpful way to gauge audience reaction to something your organization intends to share with the public. You can "pre-test" the effectiveness of your message and better determine what your audience thinks about the work and issues you present them by using focus groups and polls.

A warning: Do not fall into the trap of "social change through polls and focus groups." Many politicians have been accused of only providing leadership when the polling numbers were high instead of when the moral imperative was high. Also, focus groups and polls can be expensive and well beyond the budgets of grassroots groups.

An entire book can be written about this subject alone. Here are just a few things to be aware of.

Focus groups

In simple terms, a focus group means a collection of people who come together to focus on a specific issue or topic. Usually, a focus group consists of 6-12 people who represent your "typical audience" and whose opinions, ideas and viewpoints will help you make decisions on how to craft your media message.

Usually, focus group evaluations happen in the following manner:
■ A focus group is exposed to a "communication product" (radio program, TV spot, etc.) that contains the message.
■ A moderator leads the discussion and helps guide focus group members to freely and openly exchange ideas and to clarify viewpoints.
■ A recorder assists the moderator by taking notes and handling the video or audio taping of the session.
■ Sometimes other observers watch the proceedings through two-way mirrored windows to detect body language and other "cues" of the participants.

Like all good media planning, the **first step** to focus group research requires that you think about your outcome—where you want to be at the end of your focus group evaluations and what you want to do with the information you discover. The **second steps** are logistical ones—establishing a guide for discussions, training moderators, selecting a location and participants and determining how much incentive you will offer your participants. The **third step** is tabulating and interpreting your findings, and finally, the fourth is to report and make use of your findings.

Focus groups require significant skills and professional "detachment" from the issue. That is why most focus groups retain outside consultants to do the focus group evaluations. This can be expensive, but the research will be more unbiased and professionally produced.

The benefit of focus group evaluations is that they allow you to assess the quality of the program, message or product you are planning to release to the public. With proper planning and execution, focus groups can help you ascertain what method of

David Smith
Communicatons Director
Human Rights Campaign
1101 14th St., NW, Ste. 200
Washington, DC 20005
(P) 202 628-4160
(F) 202 347-5323
(E) hrc@hrc.org
www.hrc.org

The Human Rights Campaign (HRC), a national gay and lesbian rights organization offers the following example on how focus group evaluations helped them with message delivery. David Smith, communications director for HRC, recounted the following story:

Shortly after the Oklahoma City bombing, the news media repeatedly referred to militia groups as "radical right organizations." This term "radical right" had been used by us and allied organizations to describe groups like the Christian Coalition, Family Research Council and the like. We were afraid that the public was no longer going to accept the term "radical right" as an adequate description. The Christian Coalition is bad news, but hardly a militia (though I know some people might disagree with that).

So we at HRC embarked on a focus group and polling project to determine the right words to describe these groups that would serve to continue to discredit them and keep them on the margins of the political world. We found that a majority of the public was very uncomfortable with the notion of religion and politics mixing and was even more uncomfortable when you added extremism to the mix. The term "religious political extremist" came from that focus group work. While the term is cumbersome, and not often used, the information gleaned from the research informs how we describe and talk about groups that are on the extreme right of the political spectrum but don't dress in combat fatigues and carry assault weapons.

message delivery and what message content works best with your intended audience. They help you determine even what words and phrases resonate most with audiences.

In other words, you are learning how to position your organization and figuring out what to say and to whom. In essence, you are conducting a quality assessment campaign—but in a small and moderately controlled environment. The results should be rewarding to your ability to develop and deliver messages.

The downside of focus groups is they are not scientific, and frequently expensive. Although they may forecast well by telling you how people feel and addressing questions you have not asked, focus group evaluations do not work well with larger populations, or in situations where quantity matters.

Preparations for focus groups are rather involved. Again focus groups are complex and almost always require professional help. Contract with experienced facilitators who will handle all the details (see "Resources," page 109).

Polling

Unlike focus group evaluations, polling is more scientific and systematic. Polls are quantitative research—the measurement of and interrelationship between attitudes, beliefs and attributes. We hear about them all the time. News organizations are constantly releasing results of public opinion polling on any given number of topics, and so, polls are important to keep them in mind when doing media work. Oftentimes, polling results can help you develop your media messages and, in some cases, turn in a news item themselves.

Celinda Lake
President and Founder
Lake, Snell, Perry & Associates
1730 Rhode Island Avenue,
NW, Suite 400
Washington, DC 20036
(P) 202 776-9066
(F) 202 776-9064
(E) hrc@hrc.org
www.lakesnellperry.com

Celinda Lake, author of *Public Opinion Polling: A Handbook for Public Interest and Citizen Advocacy Groups*, outlines four major basic types of polls that will allow you to find out what people think and know and what people are like. These four types of polls include: in-depth surveys, short polls, tracking polls and panel polls.

Each allows you to get an idea of public perception over time or during a particular moment. In-depth surveys ask involved questions and seek to get a profound understanding of an issue. Short polls do the opposite and only briefly assess perceptions of a topic. Tracking polls look at the population, and subgroups, changing opinions over time. Panel polls go back and interview groups several times to learn how the groups, opinions change over time.

Using polls as news

While polls can be expensive, community and grassroots groups like yours can benefit from polling. Volunteers, if properly trained, can conduct effective polls and the result can be extremely rewarding. This type of work is not complex but does require careful and concerted planning. One of the biggest myths about polling, as Lake points out in her book, is that "Anyone can do a 'quick and dirty' poll."

According to David Smith of the Human Rights Campaign (HRC), most media organizations will not report on advocacy group-sponsored polling, since media conduct polls themselves. Smith says, "News outlets are inherently suspect of the questions being asked and the results. Our track record on securing news coverage specifically of our polls has been spotty."

However, while this may be the case, polls often help to bolster already existing news coverage. Recalling one of the HRC's successful experiences with polling, Smith feels strongly that "polling results help supplement a story that you're already pushing. It's very possible that you can add to a story by providing polling on any given topic that's relevant to that story."

He continues, "Two years ago, when California Representative Robert Dornan proposed a bill that would have kicked out all members of the military service that were HIV positive, the Human Rights Campaign did a spot poll with Republican and Democrat polling places and found that voters would oppose this measure. The results of that poll made it into several stories about the proposed amendment."

Another benefit of polling that Smith points out concerns C-SPAN coverage. C-SPAN often pays close attention to the release of polling results, especially for organizations based in D.C., where C-SPAN has its offices. Smith adds, "If C-SPAN cameras are available, they will generally cover such an event [press conference releasing polling data]. This allows unfiltered communication directly to your viewers."

Overall—whether you are making news with polls or not—polls can serve a larger purpose and help shape the messages and goals of an organization. Policy-makers, as Smith described, "are poll-driven whether or not we like it," and the release of polling results can influence how they think on a variety of critical issues and what they know of your organization. Polls also can allow you to grow your support base, by causing you to present ideas and frame debates in ways that will generate the most support for your issue and organization.

Being a better spokesperson
Speaking out effectively for your group

Being a good spokesperson takes practice and preparation. Spokespersons not only are messengers, but symbolize the professionalism of your organization and communicate the urgency of your issue. In some cases the spokesperson **personifies** the issue.

The key to being a good spokesperson is to have your messages in mind well before standing in front of a camera or microphone, and long before the interview with the reporter. Self-confidence, poise, composure and focus must come together.

In most organizations, the executive director and key staff are responsible for being spokespersons. Leadership of your board of directors can also be called upon to speak on behalf of the group. Community members affiliated with your organization might also act as spokespersons.

Whoever is your designated media spokesperson, here are a few basic tips to follow:

✓ Remember: You have something important to say and you want people to listen. Build up your self-confidence and command attention.

✓ Image is 90 percent of the game. Appear poised, in control and knowledgeable. Take a deep breath and ground yourself; try to relax.

✓ Have your key messages in mind *before* the interview. Add something personal at the beginning of your soundbite to break the barrier between you and the audience. For example, you could say, "As a working mother..." or "As a native of this community who fished this river as a boy..."

✓ Do not be thrown off by reporters' questions, no matter what they ask. Discipline the message. Turn the question back to your key messages.

✓ Do not try to explain *everything* in your soundbite or interview. This will frustrate you, confuse the reporter and overwhelm the audience. Stay on your key messages.

✓ If you goof, it is OK. Ask the reporter to go again—unless, of course, it is live radio or TV.

✓ Practice, practice, practice. But if you do mess up your soundbite, do not worry; the movement will not collapse.

A reminder about being in the media, your goals and the bottom line

• Being in the press as a community representative automatically bestows importance on you. Some activists have reported that when they walk into a meeting room the next day after appearing on TV or quoted in the newspaper, people pay more attention to them.

• Always remember that your political and cultural goals drive your media actions, not the other way around. Sometimes in the whirlwind of media coverage there is a tendency to lose sight of your goals just to make sure you are in the press. The media can be seductive this way.

• Never sell your community short in the media by betraying your goals and forsaking your accountability to the community. Decisions will sometimes have to be made on the fly and statements delivered immediately and on deadline. There will be no time to check with "the community." But always set your sights high and do not compromise the principles and goals of your campaign in the heat of media debate. Stay on message. Always be mindful about how you are representing your community and how spokespeople are automatically perceived as community leaders.

Who are your spokespersons?

Sometimes the messenger is just as important as the message. That is why it is critical to learn how to be a more effective spokesperson yourself and develop skills among people in your community so they too can be more effective messengers. The best spokespersons are those who command media attention, present a poised, confident and persuasive image and stay on message—no matter what is happening around them.

Reporters, rushing against deadlines, often do not have time to call a dozen different people looking for quotes. They tend to go with the designated spokesperson. It is important to identify key spokespersons and make those individuals available to reporters. We suggest giving key reporters the home and cell-phone numbers of your top spokespersons.

There are two kinds of spokespersons you should designate:

Organizational leaders

These spokespersons officially represent your group and can speak to any issue of relevance. This typically includes your executive director, key program staff or board co-chairs. These spokespersons should be comfortable speaking to the media, trusted to say the right thing, and have a command of the issues so they can provide reliable, accurate and timely information to reporters—or know where to get it. Reporters may call these people at any time for a quote or background information. Make sure members of the media know how and where to find these folks, including personal contact information if appropriate.

Community spokespeople

It is important to diversify your list of spokespersons so the same one or two people are not always being quoted. This is to ensure the voices of people directly affected by the issue are included in the media. Moreover, be mindful of all the kinds of diversity—racial, age, sexual orientation, ability and disability, class and gender—that make up the rich texture of your communities, and whether those people are being groomed for the media. Typically, community spokespeople are asked to speak at press conferences, rallies and other public events or write opinion editorials or appear on talk shows. Community spokespeople represent the "real people." Their dramatic personal stories can be tremendously persuasive.

Once you have identified your spokespersons, train them and get them on message. First, make sure every spokesperson has the talking points or message page on an issue. Then conduct a role-play session in which you fire questions at them. Finally, critique their responses. Set up a video camera, tape them and play the tape back. The more practice your spokespersons get, the better they become.

Case study

Spokespersons
Staff or community members?

A dilemma facing many grassroots groups is the question of who should be the group's official spokesperson(s). Most organizations have designated staff authorized to speak to the press on behalf of the organization. This typically includes program staff, legal staff, the executive director and/or key board members. This is the most convenient model for reporters because it means they can make just one call to get what they need on deadline. Other groups use different models. One grassroots organization, Kentuckians for the Commonwealth (KFTC), has a policy that allows only its community members to speak to the press for quotation.

Jerry Hardt
Media Director
Kentuckians for the Com-
monwealth
P.O. Box 697
Salyersville, KY 41465
(P) 606 349-4860
(F) 606 349-2109
(E) jhardt@foothills.net

In either case—staff vs. members as spokespersons—the key is to always be a resource for reporters and to provide them with accurate information by deadline. And no matter who the messenger is, always stay on message.

Following are the words of Jerry Hardt, media director of KFTC

—Seeta Peña Gangadharan

What is the issue?

KFTC is a statewide citizens and social justice organization working for a new balance of power and a just society. It is a member-controlled nonprofit organization with more than 2,000 members statewide. We have worked on a variety of issues, including: water contamination resulting from mining and oil and gas drilling; hazardous and solid waste issues; landowners' rights; low-income utility issues; protection of forests; welfare and economic justice; the role of money in politics; and a wide range of local issues.

Choosing who speaks for our group and for our issues has been incredibly important to us since our inception in 1981. We have held a firm policy that staff does not talk to the media, except on background. We—meaning myself as media director and the rest of the staff—are not the ones to be quoted, despite the fact that we talk to the media all the time.

This policy represents who we are as a grassroots-run organization. We feel this policy allows us to put a real human face on an issue, thus emphasizing the dramatic personal angle to the story. It also empowers our members—many of who are rarely, if ever, included in public debate—and increases the diversity of voices heard in the media.

What works: Empowering community members

Our staff prepares lists of spokespersons on a variety of issues KFTC is pursuing. These lists are provided to reporters.

We train people on the message and how to stay on it. We also prep them to anticipate reporters' questions, including tricky or sensitive inquiries. We practice beforehand, often role-playing in whatever situation we can—sometimes on the phone the night before the press conference or in the car on the way to the event. We have conducted media training sessions for members, even putting them on videotape and critiquing their performance.

To build a spokesperson's confidence, we try to put people in non-threatening situations first. For example, we may assign a member to report on a meeting for staff and other members, thus allowing her or him to practice standing up in front of a group and talking. Or, it may mean testifying to a friendly committee in the legislature before going into a hostile session.

Often, our spokespersons are able to lend certain emotions to an issue that a

continued on next page

continued from previous page

distanced person may not. If I said to a reporter, "This coal mine is threatening people's homes," it differs remarkably from a member saying, "I'm afraid to sleep at night because there is a strip mine underneath me. I never know if my house is going to cave in or not." Real people who are personally affected can convey things in a way that other spokespersons cannot.

The challenges

A challenge for us is coordination. We must coordinate the schedules of each spokesperson. Often our members are at work when reporters are available. We will provide background to the reporter, then triage calls and set up interviews as best we can. We know how to locate a person and often make the arrangements for the reporter and the member. As staff, we have to be ready to connect our members up with reporters. That way we can effectively say: "You want to do a story on logging? Here are three people to call who are personally affected by the issue and have dramatic stories to tell."

When talking to reporters, we often tell them, "If you don't have any luck connecting with our spokespersons, please call us back." Many of our members live in rural Kentucky. Sometimes we end up tracking down a cousin or an aunt, saying, "Do you know where so-and-so is?" If the reporter is on a tight deadline, we may have to scramble fast.

This requires patience on our part and understanding by reporters, some of whom want the simple one-stop-shopping phone call to get all their information. We try not to make reporters jump through hoops. They do not have the time. Our experience is that when the system works, many reporters appreciate a real-person anecdote combined with background from our staff.

A second challenge is to get our group's name in the story when a member speaks to the reporter. For example, there was a bill in the last legislative session that improved access to education for low-income Kentuckians. Originally it was a non-story for the media. But through our spokesperson efforts, we reframed the issue, put a dramatic human-interest angle on the story, and received particularly good coverage. The only problem was that while our members were quoted a lot, there were hardly any references to KFTC!

How can we improve?

We need to make our spokespersons more aware of drawing KFTC into the conversation—particularly when a reporter calls on the phone or stops someone on the steps of the capital building. There were a couple of times when spokespersons were simply credited in the media as a "welfare mother and single parent of two" or "large landowner." Our staff responded by thanking the reporter, but saying: "The two people you talked to are KFTC members and were really speaking as KFTC spokespersons. If you could include that detail next time, we'd really appreciate it."

Concluding thoughts

At our organization, we work on leadership development and our leadership base. Our spokesperson training is just one part of that effort. The hope is that if people gain these skills—even if they don't stay involved in KFTC—they can continue to put these skills to good use. Our members feel as if they have access to the media. I think our members enjoy their relationship with the media. It may cause us some logistical nightmares, but we believe it presents a truer image of the organization and is more effective in the long run. Using community spokespeople just makes sense. Empowering individuals—one of our organizational goals—means speaking for yourself.

—Jerry Hardt

3. Moving the message

Using this section to plan your media

In the previous sections we focused on the basics, framing issues, and how to construct and discipline your messages. Now, the time has come to communicate your messages to the media. That means making news. That means planning your media efforts.

Too often our efforts to make news are (a) reactive (responding to developments usually caused by opponents) or (b) hodgepodge and uncoordinated (thus resulting in missed media opportunities).

This section, the largest in the book, details the components of a successful media plan. Everything from producing press kits to writing media advisories to staging media events. First, we lay out a suggested media plan we hope you will use for your organization or issue. Then we elaborate on each point to give you the tools to engage reporters and move your messages.

At times you may undertake these activities piecemeal; for example, placing an opinion editorial without staging a media event. However, the more you can take the time to plan your media activities in advance and coordinate the many pieces, the better off you will be in terms of maximizing limited media resources, seizing media opportunities and proactively influencing debate.

Note

Steps 1 through 6 of the media plan are what you do **before** you even call a reporter or stage a media event. Once you do these, it is time to unleash the other components of your media plan.

Steps 7 to 12 are the most labor-intensive pieces of the media plan; they should be delegated accordingly. However, there should always be one person who oversees the execution of the plan and is the main contact for the media. Pitching reporters— step 7—is critical and involves intensive phone work and "schmoozing." How many of these steps can be accomplished depends on the resources of the group.

The media plan

The central theme of this guidebook is the importance of strategically planning your media. For too long our side of the battle has ignored the media, conducted media actions half-heartedly and at the last minute, or been in a constant reactive mode, thus letting our opponents frame the issue and move the message while we scramble to play catch-up. Sometimes even when we do the best job we can, we still do not get the coverage we deserve. No matter what, we still must plan our media.

Here at the SPIN Project we understand your resources are limited and your task is huge. Create your media plan *before* you launch your campaign. Conceive the plan at the same time you prepare your organizing or electoral campaign plan. Above all, do not wait until the last minute to decide to crank out a press release or call a reporter. You will most likely find yourself very frustrated. Plan for your media! This will make you proactive instead of simply reactive.

A word about reality-based media plans: Do not set yourself up for failure. Create a media plan that you and your staff can actually complete. Think big and act ambitiously, but do not overextend yourself. Doing media can be labor intensive.

Planning your media

The key components of a successful, basic media plan are:

1 **Frame** the issue. And in the process, identify your news. Remember, the best media plans will not be successful unless you have real news to make *(see "Framing the news," page 22)*.

2 **Define** messages. Write your "talking points" *(see "A model for your messages," page 29)*.

3 **Target** the audience *(see "Targeting your audience," page 20)*.

4 **Identify and train** spokesperson(s) to be on message *(see "Who are your spokespersons?," page 34)*.

5 **Target** reporters and media outlets. Create or augment your media database *(see "Developing relationships with reporters," page 39)*.

6 **Produce** your "deliverables": press kits, media advisories, press releases, fact sheets, "sign on" letters of support, informational report and other handouts *(see "News releases," page 44)*.

7 **Pitch** reporters to cover the story *(see "Pitching your story to the press," page 52)*.

8 **Conduct** media briefings for key reporters *(see "Organizing successful media briefings," page 56)*.

9 **Stage** media events *(see "Staging media events," page 60)*.

10 **Place** opinion editorials and letters to the editor *(see "Opinion editorials and letters to the editor," page 71)*.

11 **Book** spokespersons on radio and TV shows *(see "You're on the air," page 75)*.

12 **Don't** forget the Internet *(see "Using the Internet," page 78)*.

Most of this section of the guidebook elaborates on the components of a media plan. Steps 1 through 4 were covered in the previous section.

Developing relationships with reporters

Cultivate personal relationships with reporters. This is one of the most important tasks an activist can do when it comes to making news. In his book, *Making the News: A Guide for Nonprofits and Activists* (Westview Press, 1998), Jason Salzman quotes a reporter from a major daily whose sentiments are probably echoed by journalists everywhere: "A lot of what gets covered depends on personal relationships at the paper." Can't get more explicit than that.

Here are some tips for strengthening relationships with individual reporters and expanding and prioritizing your media database:

Be a resource for reporters. Develop a reputation as someone who has accurate information, meets deadlines and is able to offer a good soundbite. Provide other contacts for the reporter, even from the other side if requested.

Be accessible to reporters. They will usually try to get you on one phone call. If they cannot find you, they will often move on to other sources. Give reporters your direct line—plus your home number to key media. Carry a pager or cellular phone, especially at media events where a reporter might be calling you to get the news as it is being made. One group scored extra television coverage simply because an editor, scrounging for news on a slow day, phoned an activist at a rally to get a quote. Before the activist hung up, she had persuaded the editor to send a news crew to cover the event.

Always be prepared to say something about an issue when a reporter calls. A reporter never likes to hear, "I'll get back to you in 10 minutes." They may not have 10 minutes to spare or you might not get back to them on time. Clever, fast-thinking activists can spin off a soundbite at will. It takes practice, but you get good at it.

If you don't know the answer, offer alternatives. If you absolutely do not know the answer to a reporter's questions—especially technical or factual inquiries—say the following: "I don't know that information. I will find out and get back to you immediately. What is your deadline?" Then get back to the reporter on time. You may also offer one or two other expert sources for the reporter's rolodex.

Know your facts. Your reputation rises gloriously or crashes ignominiously depending on the accuracy of the information you give reporters. Never give reporters inaccurate or even questionably accurate information.

Do not call reporters just to be quoted. Sometimes you may be a major source for a reporter and still not be quoted. It is frustrating but those are the breaks. If you feel the omission of you or your group substantially affects the story, call that to the reporter's attention. But remember, reporters are wary of sources who whine about not being quoted all the time. Be a resource even if it means you might not be in the story. Maybe next time you will be featured.

Do not waste reporters' time. In other words, don't be a schmooze hog. This is tacky and will tarnish your reputation. Only contact reporters when you have newsworthy information, a good pitch or are responding to an inquiry or a story. Some reporters keep a mental list of news pests, media "sluts" and other obnoxious non-sources who aggravate them on a routine basis. Do not make that list.

Do not call to verify receipt of a press release. Many reporters loathe the caller who says, "Hi, did you get my press release?" Reporters do not have time to call everyone back to say whether or not they received the release. If you call a reporter, go ahead and pitch your story. In the course of the pitch, you can remind him about the media release and offer to send another.

Do not exaggerate. You can spin your news, but check the hyperbole. Be reasonable. Not every story pitch will be jaw-droppingly important. Reporters are primarily looking for the facts, additional contacts, your quotes to convey a sense of importance or controversy. They do not want Oscar acceptance speeches, used car salesman "act now!" pitches or screaming drama queens on the other end of the phone.

Avoid "sweeps week" on radio and TV. Leave reporters to do their other stories—typically the murder and mayhem pieces and other sensationalist or sentimental items—during rating periods. Call your local stations to find out when the sweeps week is scheduled. Try to avoid making news at that time.

Navigating the newsroom and targeting reporters

Knowing who to call and where to go in the newsroom is important information for identifying reporters who might cover your story and responding to media coverage. Of course, each newsroom is different. Some newsrooms are evolving out of the traditional "beat desk" layout and are creating a team approach in which several reporters cover multiple issues.

Get to know who works where in the newsroom. Pick up the phone, call and ask who covers what beat at your local paper. Visit the newsroom or broadcast station when they have public tours. Learn your way around the newsroom and you will become a more effective media activist.

Included here is the layout of a typical newspaper newsroom. It is a fairly streamlined hierarchical arrangement, with the publisher at the top, senior editors right below, followed by reporters and copy editors.

Television stations are similarly organized except an executive news producer will be near the top "editor" position, with associate producers and correspondents below. In television the beats are often less defined—except for key beats, such as "city hall" or the state legislature. One correspondent may cover a number of different stories in one day. Radio newsrooms are usually much smaller, with a news director at the top and individual reporters making up the ranks.

Who to call

When pitching stories or responding to coverage, it is important to remember that your first line of contact is always with the individual reporter.

If a reporter makes a mistake or misquotes you in an article, always speak directly to that reporter—not his or her editor. Only as a last resort do you escalate. This is disrespectful. Also, you rarely, if ever, will interact with the highest echelons of the media outlet—the owner, publisher or executive editor—on day-to-day coverage of your news. Your focus should be on reporters and those editors immediately above them.

By the way, if the headline to an article is way off, do not call the reporter to complain. Headlines are generally not written by the reporters who wrote the articles; they are written by news editors or copy editors. You can let the reporter know your opinion, but acknowledge the fact that someone else wrote it.

Do not call several reporters at one media outlet to pitch the same story. People in the newsroom generally know what others are doing and editors have a grip on the entire operation. Ask your key contact if she or he is interested. If not, ask who else you may call. If you do pitch another reporter at the same media outlet, let each reporter know that the other has been pitched. That way no one is caught by surprise.

Even if the story has potential in different departments—"Lifestyle," "Business" or "Metro"—always start with your key reporter contacts. If you do not have key contacts, cold-call a couple of reporters or general assignment editors and ask who would be interested.

Other newsroom figures to remember and possibly call are:

■ **Photo desk editors**. Typically, news editors or reporters will notify photographers but it never hurts to let the person staffing the photo desk know if there is a particularly good photo op.

■ **Assignment editors**. They triage coverage of stories on any given day.

■ **Ombudsman/woman**. This is the liaison between the community and the media, usually at newspapers and magazines, and often acts as the "conscience" of the paper.

■ **Copy editors**. In newspapers and magazines, copy editors often proofread, write headlines and edit stories.

■ **Fact checkers**. Often the bigger media outlets, especially magazines, will have a fact check department that verifies facts and other elements of stories. You may get a call from the fact checkers long after doing an interview, asking you to verify your name or some other pertinent fact. The fact checkers will not read the entire story to you, nor are they asking for your "approval" on the piece. Do not consider this an opportunity to "rewrite" the article for the journalist. Fact checkers are just checking the facts.

■ **Editorial and advertising departments**. These two departments are always separate, usually physically distinguished in another part of the building. However, at some media outlets the lines appear to be blurred as more "news" looks like infomercials for advertisers. If you have a complaint about an editorial, call the editorial page editor. If an advertisement warrants comment or response, call the advertising director.

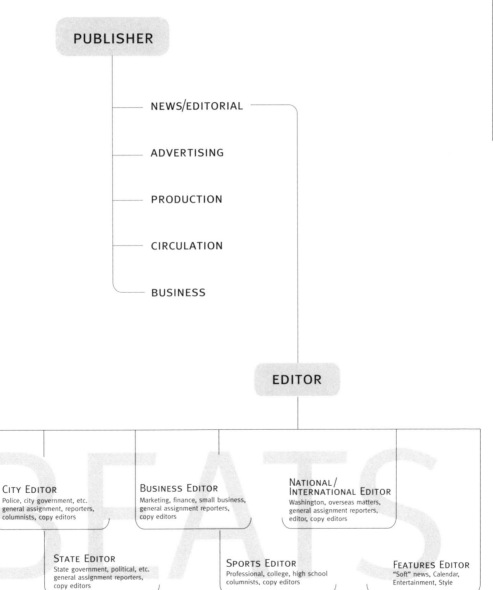

PUBLISHER

NEWS/EDITORIAL

ADVERTISING

PRODUCTION

CIRCULATION

BUSINESS

EDITOR

BEATS

CITY EDITOR
Police, city government, etc.
general assignment, reporters,
columnists, copy editors

STATE EDITOR
State government, political, etc.
general assignment reporters,
copy editors

BUSINESS EDITOR
Marketing, finance, small business,
general assignment reporters,
copy editors

SPORTS EDITOR
Professional, college, high school
columnists, copy editors

**NATIONAL/
INTERNATIONAL EDITOR**
Washington, overseas matters,
general assignment reporters,
editor, copy editors

FEATURES EDITOR
"Soft" news, Calendar,
Entertainment, Style

Expanding and prioritizing your media database

Keeping a current database of reporter contacts is hard work. Beats and reporters often change frequently. Media lists can go out-of-date by the time your mailing labels finish printing.

Still, every organization doing media work must have an organized list of reporters. Here are some suggestions for creating your database and prioritizing the reporter contacts:

■ Pay attention to "bylines": a line designating who wrote or produced the piece. Start noticing the names of journalists attached to stories—who is covering what, who favors what type of story, who is on what beat. A "beat" is a designated area or issue assigned to reporters, such as "City Hall," "Women's Beat," or "State Legislature." When watching TV or listening to the radio, write down the name of the producer or correspondent. Clip print articles and enter the byline into your database. Focus on those stories with crossover interest to your issue. You can later pitch a reporter by saying: "Last week you did that piece on so-and-so. I thought you might be interested in this story."

■ Pick up the phone, contact the media outlet, and ask what reporters or producers cover your issue. Enter the names into your database.

■ Capture the names of all reporters who contact you.

■ See the resources section *(page 109)* for contacts at media associations. Many of them sell their media lists. Also, check out the media list references such as *Bacon's Media Directories*.

■ Do not forget ethnic media, youth media, campus media, gay/lesbian/bisexual/transgender press and other constituency media.

■ Trade your growing list with those of other organizations in your area or region.

■ Add all the contact information into a database that will print in label format for mailing. More and more people are getting online, so do not forget to include e-mail addresses so you can send releases via e-mail. If you have a fax machine with broadcast fax capability, enter fax numbers for your key media. A tip for broadcast faxing: If there is no urgent time restraint on your news, fax overnight when newsroom machines are clear. But if the news is urgent and you want to get your statement out immediately, fax away!

■ When faxing reporters, do not fax every reporter in the newsroom with the same release in the hopes of hooking one reporter who will do the story. Reporters talk to each other and will be onto your game. Send releases only to your key contacts. If there are different departments or a few reporters who might be interested in your news, it is fine to send more than one release to the same news outlet.

■ Once you have developed your database, prioritize it so you can contact media in the most effective manner. You may not have the resources to personally contact all the reporters all the time.

Assuming you now have a database of about 100 reporters, you will want to:

■ Create a sub-list of your top five to 10 reporters. Develop strong personal relationships with this cluster. They get the priority treatment. Keep their names and numbers handy at all times. These are the first to get breaking news calls, pitches, press kits and briefings. Stay in regular contact with them. Have lunch or coffee with them sometime during the year.

■ The next 25 to 50 reporters on your list comprise the second tier of reporters. They get press releases faxed and mailed, at least one pitch call during the year and a heads-up on upcoming media events.

■ The third tier—the remaining 50 or so—get at least the press releases and other news material routinely sent to them.

When a reporter calls
Reporter intake form

It is important to get information from reporters when they call that you can use later when developing relationships with the press and tracking coverage. Use this "reporter intake form" to capture basic information and keep a record of exchanges and contacts. This information should be kept in a central location. Contact information—especially for new reporters—should be put into your media database.

DATE: _____

TIME (include time zone): _____

YOUR NAME/GROUP: _____

REPORTER'S NAME: _____

MEDIA OUTLET: _____

CONTACT PHONE #: _____

*FAX: _____

*E-MAIL: _____

*ADDRESS: _____
(*=If you can get it)

DEADLINE: _____

INQUIRY ABOUT:_____
(Summarize questions.)

_____

_____

_____

_____

_____

_____

YOUR RESPONSE: _____
(Summarize answers, don't forget to move the messages!)

_____

_____

_____

FOLLOW UP NEEDED? _____

STATUS? _____

_____

News releases
The who, what, where, when and why of it all

The fact: Other than the telephone, press releases and media advisories—often lumped together under the term "news releases"—are the basic methods of communicating your news to reporters.

The Reality: Reporters throw away or ignore many if not most press releases because they do not contain any news; do not have contact information or other key data to make the reporter's job easier; are filled with typos and other embarrassments, causing the reporter to doubt the integrity of the organization that sent the release; are confusing, poorly written, or worse—boring.

Reporters' desks are overflowing with news releases announcing some "big news" that really is not. Most of these are trying to sell some commercial product or event in the guise of news. Fortunately, your release, which will promote your cause, can and will distinguish itself from the others if you follow these basic tips below.

First, some definitions:

Media advisory

This is a short, one-page, concise piece *advising* the media of news to be made. Typically, a media advisory invites reporters to cover some event or press conference, or notifies them of your news. It usually contains the who, what, where, when and why of the news, including contact names, numbers and other pertinent facts. The media advisory is sent out before an event or news is made.

Press release, a.k.a. media release

This document is longer than a media advisory, but rarely more than two pages. A press release is typically written like a news story—containing quotes, "color" and background—and summarizes your news. It is written as if it were to appear in the morning newspaper—though, of course, that will not happen since most media will not run your release verbatim. The press release is often handed out at a news event or included in a press kit.

The key to successful news releases is brevity and factual accuracy. Get to the most important part of the news as soon as possible and make sure everything is accurate: facts, name spellings, dates and times. Some reporters have said that if their attention is not piqued by the headline or the end of the lead paragraph, they rarely read any further.

When to send the release

In general, you should *mail* the release 10 days before the event, *fax* it five days before the event, and follow up with a *phone* call within three days of the event. *(See "When to Call Reporters," page 52)*. Of these three methods, faxing and calling are paramount. Also, consider e-mailing the release.

Remember: Do not call reporters to ask if they got your release. They do not have time to respond to every release they receive. Instead, call them to pitch the news and remind them about the release. Be prepared to send another if the first was misplaced. Do not send multiple copies of the same release to several different reporters at one news outlet with the hope that at least *someone* will cover it. Reporters talk to one another and will be onto your game. Send only to your key contacts or call and ask who might be interested.

News release taboos

Do not include jargon or political rhetoric in your releases. There should be no mission statements in releases. Do not write in long sentences and ponderous paragraphs. One- or two-sentence paragraphs are fine. Typos, factual inaccuracies and other mistakes kill the integrity of your organization and news.

Writing news releases

Starting at the top of the page, all news releases should contain:

■ Either *For Immediate Release* —meaning the information can be used as soon as a reporter gets it—or *Embargoed* —meaning the reporter cannot use the news until the date specified (*see "Embargoes and your report," page 67*).

■ The date the release is distributed.

■ Contact name(s) and number(s), including cellular phone numbers.

■ Your organization's logo. This should be at the very top of the paper.

■ The headline is key. Most reporters have about 30 seconds to scan a news release. They want the news to jump out at them. If you do not catch their attention in the headline, into the "circular file" the release goes. Summarize your news into a headline. The headline can be up to four lines long, centered, in bold face and written all in capital letters, usually in a larger type size. You may do a stacked headline (*see "Making news with your report," page 66*). The headline should capture the larger frame of the news, communicate a sense of drama and pull reporters into the story.

Media Advisories

In media advisories, list the "Five W's"—who, what, when, where and why—after the headline and lead framing paragraph.

WHO: Who is announcing the news? This will probably be your organization or coalition. But remember, the news is not the fact that your group is announcing something, but what is being announced. Therefore, the lead paragraph will first communicate the news, then indicate who made it. A brief list of key speakers may be included here, with their names and affiliations.

WHAT: What is being announced: a media event, rally, protest, press conference or release of a new report.

WHERE: The location of the event. Include the actual address or directions, unless it is an obvious place like the steps of City Hall.

WHEN: The time—include a.m. or p.m.—and the day and make sure it corresponds with the date.

WHY: This is your key message. It is why you are making news, condensed into your messages.

If your event will feature strong visuals, as all media events should, tip reporters off to the photo opportunities at the end of the media advisory. This is particularly useful for TV.

News Releases

■ In news releases, after the headline, the first paragraph—"the lead"—is paramount. This is the summary paragraph that communicates the most important components, and frames the issue for maximum media impact. It must also capture attention. Caution: Do not try to explain *everything* in this paragraph.

■ Write the remainder of the press release in descending order of importance. In journalism, this is called the "inverted-pyramid" style of writing. The most important, base-laying news goes at the top, the lesser details below.

■ Frame your news—establish its importance and impact, and your position—by the end of the lead paragraph. At the latest, your news should be framed by the end of the second paragraph. By the third paragraph you should move your key messages (*see "Key media messages," page 26*).

■ Include one or two pithy soundbite quotes in the press release.

■ End both advisories and press releases with the marks: ###, or -30-. This lets journalists know the release is over. If your release jumps to the next page, write "more" at the bottom and center it. At the top left corner of the next page, write "Page 2" and provide a subject reference.

Press release example

COMMUNITIES FOR A BETTER ENVIRONMENT

For Immediate Release
Feb. 25, 1998

Contact: Wendall Chin, Mike Thomas
(415) 243-8373, ext. 213

EL NIÑO WREAKS HAVOC ON SAN FRANCISCO SEWAGE SYSTEM
GROUP PROTESTS "INEFFECTIVE" TREATMENT PLANT,
DEMANDS ACTION FROM CHIEF OF CITY SEWAGE

San Francisco, CA. In the middle of the worst storms in San Francisco's modern history—El Niño downpours that are causing unprecedented run-off and pollution in the bay and beaches—alarmed residents, anglers, swimmers and surfers protested outside San Francisco's sewage office, saying the new system is ineffective and must be overhauled.

Dozens of outraged residents—many from Hunter's Point, Bayview and other low-income neighborhoods—including some who fish the bay for their livelihood, protested what they called an inefficient sewage system that had problems long before El Niño. The storms are now making the situation worse, said the protesters.

"El Niño is a huge brewing problem that has implications for many people way beyond the current floods," said Wendall Chin of Communities For a Better Environment (CBE). "It is exposing the cracks in our new sewage treatment plan. The sewage plan is not effective in treating waste in San Francisco. Poisons are being dumped into the bay and beaches, endangering the lives of the people who use them the most. We need an overhaul of the system and a review of the plan for future treatment. All people in San Francisco deserve to live and work in clean, safe communities."

CBE organized the event and delivered postcards of protest from more than 20,000 families and individuals to Anson Moran, head of the Bay area's largest sewage plant. The protest was held in the wake of increased pollution caused by El Niño storms and the system's inability to handle the run-off. CBE has long challenged the new $1 billion sewage system as being ineffective, and says it particularly affects poor and other communities who must use the beaches and bay for their livelihood.

Flaws exposed by the storm waters include the severe difficulty in controlling beach pollution during harsh weather as well as in dry seasons, resulting in more beach closings than ever from dangerous levels of bacteria. The current storms are also increasing water pollution threats in low-income areas such as Bayview and Hunter's Point. CBE representatives said the sewage office does not adequately warn immigrant communities and other residents of low-income neighborhoods about water pollution threats, such as posting multilingual warning signs.

"The new $1 billion sewage facility project needs to be upgraded and key components changed," said Chin of CBE. "We are demanding an immediate meeting with Chief Moran to involve our communities so we can find a solution to this dangerous problem."

Besides changing key components of its sewage operations and design, Chin said the industrial pollution prevention program of the city must be overhauled and large, multilingual warning signs posted.

Standing in brown sud-stained water and dirty beach sand beneath umbrellas bearing the messages "Save the Beaches" and "Healthy Bay For Our Kids," protesters picketed outside the sewage plant headquarters in downtown San Francisco. Several spoke out about pollution problems they had experienced. Protesters then marched into the building to deliver bags containing thousands of postcards to the system general manager.

"We are here to speak on behalf of the more than 25,000 families who have signed the postcards of protest," said Jorge Rodriguez, a regular swimmer and fisher off Baker Beach. "I and members of my family have gotten sick from swimming, but haven't seen health warnings informing the community about dangers."

"There seems to be no real attempt at protecting public health or evaluating the health effects of the run-off," said Linda Blue of Blue Environmental Engineering, a company that specializes in sewage run-off problems. "The system needs to be changed and upgraded."

"Me and my family fish regularly in the bay. And we in the community have witnessed more and more pollution," said local angler Bill Bradley of Hunter's Point. "We are fighting today not just for better regulations, but more importantly for a better quality of life for all of us."

# # #

Contact CBE's SAFER! project at (415) 243-8373 for more information on the sewage facility and the clean bay and beach campaign.

Media advisory example

COMMUNITIES FOR A BETTER ENVIRONMENT

For Release On:
Wednesday, Feb. 25

Contact: Wendall Chin, Mike Thomas
(415) 243-8373, ext. 213

EL NIÑO WREAKS HAVOC
ON SAN FRANCISCO SEWAGE SYSTEM

GROUP DEMANDS ACTION FROM CHIEF OF CITY SEWAGE PLANT, PROTEST PLANNED

What: Bay area families and members of Communities for a Better Environment (CBE) will stage a stormy press conference and protest in front of the city sewage plant headquarters to voice their concern about the inefficient new sewage system and growing beach and bay pollution in San Francisco. Thousands of postcards will be delivered to the city Public Utilities Commission General Manager. The protest comes in the wake of increased pollution caused by El Niño storms and the system's inability to handle the run-off. CBE has long charged the new $1 billion sewage system as being ineffective, and says it particularly affects poor and other communities who must use the beaches and bay for their livelihood.

Where: Public Utilities Commission, San Francisco (Sewage Plant Administrative Headquarters), front entrance at the corner of Market and 8th Streets.

When: Wednesday, Feb. 25, 1998—12:30 p.m. press conference and protest.

Who: Sponsored by Communities for a Better Environment SAFER! Project. The protest will feature a beachgoer who has been sick because of pollution on the sands, an angler felled after eating poisoned fish caught in the bay and a surfer who developed sinus infections from sewage-infested waters. Also appearing will be an expert on treating sewage run-off caused by storms. SAFER! is a community-based advocacy project comprised of Asian, African-American, Latino and Anglo families alarmed about the health of their environment.

Why: "El Niño is a huge brewing problem that has implications for many people way beyond the current floods," said Wendall Chin of CBE. "It is exposing the cracks in our new sewage plant, which is not effective in treating waste in San Francisco. Poisons are being dumped into the bay and beaches, endangering the lives of the people who use them the most, especially the poor and communities of color who depend on fishing. We need an overhaul of the system and a review of the plan for future treatment. All people in the city deserve to live and work in clean, safe communities."

Media Visuals: Umbrellas with "stop pollution" messages; huge sand box with dirty sand, brown beach suds and debris; large container of dirty water direct from the bay; blown-up postcards.

# # #

The press kit

A good press kit can be an invaluable resource to reporters and help you shape your news. A bad press kit, one that is filled with obviously self-promotional junk or volumes of useless information stuffed into weighty notebooks, gets tossed into the "circular file."

There are two kinds of press kits for nonprofit groups:

1 A generic press kit for your group. This can be given out at any time and is not connected to one issue. It is about your identity and profile. It may contain historical information about the group, members of the board and a newsletter or annual report.

2 An issue-focused press kit. This will contain some background information about your group but mostly will feature information about a specific issue.

The beauty of a good press kit is that it can be customized and modified, some things taken out and new material inserted.

Give your press kits to reporters at briefings, press conferences or other media events. Send press kits for media events to no-show reporters.

Below is a suggested model for issue-focused press kits. This kit is contained in a nice, but not overly fancy, folder that opens up to reveal two pockets. The right pocket contains the key information.

The left pocket

✔ Fact sheets on your organization and any other major organization(s) working in conjunction with you. If two groups have sponsored the research, include a piece here on both, with contact names and numbers.

✔ Statements of support from allied groups on their letterhead. Also include a "sign-on" page, listing supportive groups.

✔ A sampling of previous press clips—your "greatest hits"—on your group or issue.

✔ Copy of any op ed you may have placed.

✔ Black and white, 5x7 or 8x10 photograph of key spokesperson(s), photo op of your event in the past or something that visualizes the issue—along with a caption. Smaller papers in particular might use the photograph. This is optional.

✔ Finally, do not forget your business card or custom-made rolodex card. Clip it to the inside pocket.

The right pocket

✔ Your main press release on the issue. This moves your messages right at the beginning. Note: If you are handing out the kit at a media event, insert the line-up of event speakers—with their names spelled correctly, contact numbers for follow-up questions and short biographies—before the press release.

✔ A copy of your statement(s) delivered at the event. If there is no event, make sure the press release contains quotes from the statement. This is a source of quotes for reporters and will move your messages.

✔ A fact sheet on the issue: one page, bullet form, just the facts. If your issue involves the release of a new report, the fact sheet will focus on your findings and summarize the report.

✔ The report. If you are releasing new research, add the full report here. An executive summary should be at the front of the report.

✔ Other fact sheets on related issues.

Press kit example

- Black and White Photo with Caption
- Copies of Best Press Clips
- Biographies of Key Speakers
- List of Supporters
- More Fact Sheet(s) on Organization

- "Report"
- Fact Sheet(s) on Issue
- Longer Statement (or Speech Text)
- Press Release

Business Card

Press Kit: This kit could be handed out at a media event or customized for other uses by adding or removing pieces.

Fact sheets

Fact sheets are simply what the name implies: just the facts. They are one-page "finger tip" fact reviews that list pertinent information, data, gee-whiz numbers, percentage numbers and so forth. Fact sheets are useful for reporters who do not have time to read entire press releases or are looking for just one tidbit of information.

▮ Title each fact sheet specific to the issue and subject. For example, "Fact sheet on abortion and young women."

▮ Print fact sheets on your organization's letterhead, including a contact name and number in the top right corner.

▮ "Bulletize" your fact sheets. Use a bullet—similar to the one at the beginning of this item—to list the facts. Include no more than one or two sentences/facts per bullet.

▮ You can always break down an issue. Having more than one fact sheet for your press kit is perfectly OK. The separate fact sheets could be on different aspects of the issue, such as history, "gee-whiz" numbers, etc.

▮ Fact sheets rarely include lengthy quotes or anecdotes—just the facts. This means percentage numbers, statistical breakdowns, numerical "ups-and-downs," charting trends or changes, historical narratives, biographical facts, monetary figures and conclusions of research can all be included in your fact sheets.

▮ A word about percentages: Translate them into something that is easy to visualize. For example, "30 percent" would be "almost one out of three," or "50 percent" is "half."

▮ Fact sheets are never longer than one page. Keep them short and simple.

▮ Include your fact sheets in your press kit (*see "The press kit" page 48*), or hand them out individually to reporters who need the information. Make certain the facts are updated and accurate.

Fact sheet example

Young women and abortion

Young women belonging to the post-Roe v. Wade generations have never known illegal abortion. They tend to take abortion for granted, seeing it as something they're entitled to, not something to fight for. Although 55 percent of all women who seek abortions are under 25[1], young women are often unaware of the obstacles to services that are created by restrictions on abortion.

Susan Yanow
Executive Director
Abortion Access Project
552 Massachusetts Ave., Ste. 215
Cambridge, MA 02139
(P) 617 661-1161
(F) 617 492-1915
(E) info@repro-activist.org
www.repro-activist.org

■ **Many young women face unplanned pregnancies, despite increased contraceptive use.** Nationally, 9 in 10 sexually active women and their partners use a contraceptive method, although not always consistently or correctly.[2] 76 percent of women used contraception at first intercourse in the 1990s, compared with 50 percent before 1980.[3] But contraception is not foolproof: 6 out of 10 women who seek abortions experienced contraceptive failure.[4]

■ **Each year, almost one million teenage women—11 percent of all women aged 15-19 and 20 percent of those who have had sexual intercourse—become pregnant.** 78 percent of teen pregnancies are unplanned, accounting for of all accidental pregnancies annually.[2] Nearly 4 in 10 teen pregnancies (excluding miscarriages) end in abortion.[2] 55 percent of U.S. women obtaining abortions are younger than 25: Women aged 20-24 obtain 33 percent of all abortions, and teenagers obtain 22 percent.[1]

In Massachusetts in 1996, women under 25 accounted for 44 percent (12,843) of all abortions. Girls 14 and under had 148 abortions; 15-19 years had 4,465; 20-24 years had 8230.[5]

■ **Restrictions on abortion disproportionately affect teenage women.** 39 states, including Massachusetts, have parental involvement laws on the books for abortion. These laws are enforced in 31 states.[6] 61 percent of teens having abortions do so with at least one parent's knowledge.[2] Yet 27 states and the District of Columbia have laws that specifically authorize a pregnant minor to obtain prenatal care and delivery services without parental notification,[7] representing a double standard in our commitment to young women's health.

■ **Young women are unaware of obstacles to health care created by restrictions on abortion.** In 1998 the Pro-Choice Public Education Project (PEP) conducted polls with young women across the country. The PEP poll found that a majority of young women support the availability of legal abortion and consider themselves pro-choice. However, young women are often unaware of how restrictions such as parental involvement laws, a shortage of providers, a lack of funding, biased counseling requirements and mandatory waiting periods can interfere with their ability to exercise the right to choose abortion. The Real Women, Real Choices Campaign is designed to educate young women and the public about the impact of these restrictions.

1 Alan Guttmacher Institute, "Induced Abortion," 1996.
2 Ibid. "Teen Sex and Pregnancy," 1998.
3 Ibid. "Contraceptive Use," 1998.
4 Ibid. "Facts in Brief: Induced Abortion," 1996.
5 Massachusetts Department of Public Health Bureau of Health Statistics Research & Evaluation, 1997.
6 NARAL, "Who Decides: A State-by-State Review of Abortion and Reproductive Rights, 1998.
7 Alan Guttmacher Institute, "Teenagers' Right to Consent to Reproductive Healthcare," 1997.

When to call reporters

Pitching a story is sometimes as much about timing as it is about framing and luck. Here are tips for when to call a reporter.

■ Do not call reporters when you know they are on deadline. If you do get through to them they will be irritated and try to get you off the phone fast. A reporter working on the next morning's paper will be crashing on deadline any time after 3:30 p.m. the day before. Television reporters most likely will be out of reach up to an hour before they go on the air. So if your local evening news starts at 5 p.m., avoid calling reporters after 3:00 or 3:30 p.m. This of course does not apply if really big news is breaking. Then call! And sometimes radio reporters, if they can confirm the story (through wire service coverage, for example), might put it on immediately (that is one of the beauties of radio news—it often is the first on a fast-breaking story).

■ Late morning, say, around 10:30 a.m., is a good time to call reporters. They have already had their morning coffee, their daily planning meetings probably have concluded, and it is before they get deeply involved in other stories. The earlier in the week the better.

■ It is not advised to call on a weekend unless some big news is breaking or you have an event unfolding and you are checking to see if the media outlet is sending anyone (presuming you have already sent them the media advisory and pitched the event). Weekend shifts might mean you may not have regular contact with the reporter and thus they may not know you or the issue. On the other hand, if your regular reporter contact is not around, pitch anyone who is interested.

Pitching your story to the press

A colleague once summed up the importance of pitching with a small sign he posted in the midst of a particularly demanding media campaign: "It's the follow-up call, stupid." In other words, no matter how brilliant your message or clever your frame, it can very well be irrelevant if you do not follow through with the pitch call.

Pitching means "selling" your news story to a reporter or editor. It typically is done over the phone, although reporters can be pitched in person at briefings or while they are covering other events.

Making the pitch call is something like telemarketing. You are calling someone who is probably busy and distracted—in this case a reporter or editor—in an attempt to sell them something when they probably do not sound very interested. It can be nerve-wracking.

We have all been interrupted during dinner by a telemarketer from yet another credit card or long-distance phone company. And we probably all have attempted to hang up as quickly as possible. On occasion, we might have spoken with the person for a few minutes—even if we did not buy the product.

Think about why you may have gruffly hung up on one caller yet listened courteously to another. Most likely, the caller who got your attention sounded *human*: relaxed, articulate and genuine about the reason for the call. The callers most easy to hang up on, on the other hand, probably sounded like they were reading from a script, droning on despite your protestations about being in the middle of dinner.

Believe it or not, your experience *answering* the phone will help you when it is time to begin calling reporters. Often, you will have no more than a few minutes to convince the person you have news. Here are some tried and true rules to bear in mind while your fingers do the walking and your mouth does the pitching.

How to Pitch

Offer reporters something they need
Come rain or shine, the news goes on day after day. The press is always in need of a good story—and you are in a position to give it to them. Half the success of the pitch call depends on your confidence level; the rest will follow with your messages and how you frame the issue. Remember, you need media coverage and the reporter needs news. However, do not waste anyone's time; pitch the press only when you have news.

Keep it brief
Reporters do not have time for long-winded calls. You will have only a few minutes to get their attention and capture their interest immediately. Make certain your pitch contains the who, what, where, when and why. Do not call simply to ask if they received your media advisory. Pitch the story, reference the media advisory or release and offer to send it again if they have not seen it.

Begin with reporters you know
Target specific reporters with whom you have relationships. If they have done a piece on your issue or a similar subject, reference their prior work: "Hi, that terrific piece you wrote last month made me think you might be interested in what's happening next week." At the very least, target reporters in the relevant section of the paper. Pick a section based on how you are framing the news and call the appropriate reporter. If you must make a cold call, ask the general assignment editor or producer who you should contact; then call that reporter.

Offer a hook
There are many tricks for making your story tantalizing: dramatic human interest, controversy, local angles, calendar tie-ins, anniversaries and other major events. Frame the story so it has greater significance, drama, timeliness and impact for more readers, viewers and listeners. The better you frame your news, the better the pitch, the greater your chances of scoring a media hit. Remember, even if you spark the reporters' interest they still may have to sell the idea to the editors. So, help reporters out with better hooks and frames (see "Framing for our lives," page 24).

Express enthusiasm
When it comes to pitching, you will be competing with a long list of other callers. If you are not excited about the story, the reporter will not be excited either. However, do not go overboard with your enthusiasm. Give reporters the necessary information, offer to provide more and get off the phone.

Be timely, not obnoxious
Do not call reporters when you know they are on deadline. If you get them at all, they will probably try to get you off the phone immediately. Mid-morning and early afternoon are good times to make the pitch. Also, be sensitive to reporters' moods. If you sense they are rushed, offer to call back later. At the very least, acknowledge their predicament: "Listen, I know you're very busy; do you have a moment or should I call back later?"

Close the deal
Ask reporters if they are interested in your event and whether they can come. Most will not immediately commit over the phone but will think about it. They then must pitch their editors.

Have one or two back-up pitch angles
If it becomes clear that a reporter is not interested, consider a different angle. Perhaps he cannot attend a media event, but would be interested in interviewing one of the speakers at another time. A reporter might respond more favorably to the human-interest angle of a story rather than the political-controversy or business angle.

More pitch tips
- Do not pitch more than one reporter at a news outlet. If you do talk to more than one reporter, let them know.
- Emphasize the visuals, especially for television.
- If you get voice mail, leave the basic information and call back. Pitch the answering machine!
- If the reporter you call is not interested or on another beat, ask whom you can speak to instead.

Phone pitch example

This actual phone pitch has a good hook (El Niño), a strong frame (lots of people affected) and a direct approach that informs the reporter. This pitch probably took all of three minutes.

CBE: "Hi, this is Wendall Chin from Communities for a Better Environment calling. I know you're very busy, but I wanted to take just a moment to tell you about an exciting event happening next week regarding El Niño."

REPORTER: "Yeah, what is it. I can't talk long."

CBE: "We faxed over a media advisory this morning for our protest next week in front of the San Francisco sewage director's office. We are conducting a protest to expose the inadequacies of the new $1 billion sewage system. You've written a story about how beaches up and down the California coast are being closed because of polluted run-off caused by the storms. Well, the same thing is threatened here, but even bigger. The storms are exposing the problems with the inferior sewage plan, problems that may have dire and controversial consequences long after El Niño leaves. Our new sewage system is already failing Mother Nature's test. It must be overhauled."

REPORTER: "That sounds interesting; tell me more."

CBE: "We are presenting thousands of postcards signed by concerned residents of San Francisco to the chief of sewage and we are demanding an urgent meeting with him. The polluted run-off not only threatens nearby tourist beaches, but in particular it affects low-income people who fish the Bay for their livelihood. Everyone suffers because of the problem. The protest will be Wednesday, Feb. 25, at 12:30 p.m. in front of the sewage office at 1155 Market Street near 7th Street."

REPORTER: "Do you have background on this problem?"

CBE: "Yes, we've got facts on the closings of the beach and a fact sheet on the sewage plan, which we think is seriously deficient. El Niño is a huge problem that has implications way beyond the publicized stories of homes falling into the sea. The sewage system has cracks that we have been trying to fix for years. It's hurting the community by allowing sewage to overflow onto the beaches and into the Bay. Thousands of families are outraged, and El Niño is making it worse."

REPORTERS: "What's going to happen at the protest?"

CBE: "We will present the postcards signed by outraged families. There will be exciting visuals of storm umbrellas stenciled with messages, dirty sand and brown suds from the closed beaches, and protesters in "hazardous material" uniforms with beach balls and fishing poles. Does this sound like something you would cover?"

REPORTER: "Uh, maybe. I'll check with my editor."

CBE: "Great. We hope you can cover it. Let me know if you need more information. Thank you."

—Wendall Chin

Wendall Chin
Lead Organizer
Communities for a Better Environment
500 Howard Street, Ste. 506
San Francisco, CA 94105
(P) 415 243-8373
(F) 415 243-8980
(E) cbebucket@igc.org
www.igc.org/cbesf

Pitching an exclusive

The "exclusive." You have probably seen or read one, perhaps beginning something like this: "And now for an exclusive XYZ News report on the link between smoking and cancer." "Exclusive" generally means the media outlet reporting the story is the only outlet reporting it at this time. So, even if it is a huge story—"Senator Resigns; Corporate Payoffs Uncovered"—you will not see it elsewhere by flipping the channel or picking up a different newspaper, at least not right away. It will quickly be picked up by other media outlets; in the case of television, sometimes even on the same day.

There are two types of exclusive. There is the story that a particular news organization or reporter "uncovers"—say Watergate—that only they have. And there is the exclusive that an organization gives to a specific reporter or media outlet— to the *exclusion* of other press.

For example, you have a major report coming out on dangerous levels of lead found in your city's elementary schools. Your group's reports have historically not gotten great coverage and you want to make sure this report makes a big splash. You particularly want to target the state legislature, which is in the middle of budget negotiations. As a result, the most important media "hit" will be your regional daily paper, which is widely read by policy-makers across the state.

To better insure your chance of getting the coverage you need, you may send the newspaper an advance copy of the report. In this case it is important to set an official release date—whether or not you end up granting an exclusive—and stamp all copies of your report with this "embargo" date. Therefore, reporters can use the material to begin writing their story, but they cannot run it until your release date. In the case of granting an exclusive, however, you may give a particular paper or news program the OK to break the story a day early. Sounds complicated, right?

Make no mistake. Pitching and granting an exclusive can be very tricky and offer *no* guarantee that you will receive the ideal coverage. For this reason, it is generally a tactic that you want to employ under limited circumstances. Ideally, your particular story will break in a number of your desired media outlets simultaneously. However, the reasons you may consider granting an exclusive include:

■ **Limited time and resources.** You need to get your story out quickly and you have a very narrow target audience—say, policy-makers and business leaders. In such a case, you might approach only the business section of your paper. If it is a hot story, other outlets will come to you once it runs.

■ **A definite need for high-profile coverage.** You have had trouble getting on the evening news in the past. For tactical reasons you decide that you cannot afford to be shut out this time so you offer the exclusive upfront.

■ **It is your best bargaining chip.** You finally set up a meeting with a reporter for an important outlet, who is interested in the story, but non-committal about what she can do. You let her know that other outlets are interested, but you are willing to give her the exclusive. Now she has something to take back to her editor and a stake in the story.

Granting an exclusive

1. Make sure you ask about placement. You do not want to give away the story for two paragraphs on page B26 or for 30 seconds at the end of the newscast. It is a negotiation, so be sure to make clear what you are expecting out of the deal.

2. Be careful of double dealing. Playing reporters off one another is a risky business and can ruin your relationship for years to come. Do not approach a second news organization until the first one has declined on the story. And be absolutely clear about the terms of your agreement.

3. Be ready for other media to be mad at you, particularly smaller outlets that hate it when you help the big fish scoop them.

4. Remember, information really prefers to be free. Use exclusives with the utmost discretion.

Organizing successful media briefings and editorial board reviews

Media briefings and editorial board reviews are important ways to educate reporters, producers and editors about your news and give them a deeper understanding of your issue. They are also a good way to turn around bad coverage or negative editorials. You should consider editorial board reviews as part of your media plan.

Most journalists welcome the opportunity to be briefed, as long as you have news and are not wasting their time. Editorial review boards of major newspapers—usually comprised of all section editors—welcome the opportunity to engage in dialogue with reputable community groups, even those with whom they often disagree. You should consider scheduling a briefing once or twice a year with your major local daily newspaper or key TV/radio stations.

Media briefings vs. editorial board reviews

A **media briefing** is typically held with reporters, editors and producers. These are the people who will cover your issue as news or as features. Media briefings are conducted to pitch news stories, educate the news staff about the issue and upcoming events or challenge biased or inaccurate news coverage.

An **editorial board review** is held with the governing body of editorial writers and editors who guide the editorial "voice" of the paper. Editorial board reviews are conducted to persuade the media outlet to take an editorial position on your issue or run your op ed, or to challenge regularly biased editorials.

Note: The editorial staff—those who manage the editorial pages, including editorials, op eds and letters—is typically separate from the newsroom staff.

The following tips focus primarily on media briefings, though the ideas offered here can easily be applied to an editorial board review. The following case study on editorial review board meetings goes into detail about setting up meetings with the editorial staff.

Preparations for the briefing

1 Schedule the briefing

Typically, briefings are held before lunch, after the morning newsroom staff meetings. They are often scheduled for early or mid-week. Call the managing editor, key reporter contact or section editor to schedule the briefing. Schedule a briefing only when you have news of significant impact or about a major issue with the media outlet, such as ongoing bias. Do not request a briefing simply to inform them of the opening of your new office or hiring new staff, for example. Instead, you should use the briefing to inform, educate and pitch broader stories or provide background on emerging news. Briefing sessions usually last less than two hours.

2 Identify appropriate reporters

Think of reporters, editors and producers who should attend and invite them. These might include:
✔ "Beat" reporters covering your issue.
✔ Reporters with whom you have developed relationships.
✔ Political reporters.
✔ News editors.

✔ "Page" editors: religion, editorial, state news, lifestyle, etc.
✔ Managing and/or executive editors.
✔ Radio/TV producer and executive news producers and correspondents.

Before the briefing

3 Prepare "deliverables" to hand out at the briefing
▪ Press kit—even if they already received one in the mail.
▪ Contact information of participants and organizations.
▪ Clips of previous coverage.
▪ Background fact sheets on issues.
▪ List of additional contacts.
▪ List of story ideas.

4 Identify who from your group should attend
These include, but are not limited to: executive director, staff, board members, community members, issue experts, author of news-making report to be released, individuals personally affected by issue. Keep the number manageable—no more than five.
▪ "Rehearse" briefing with your side's participants beforehand.
▪ Identify lead speaker to start briefing.
▪ Assign role to each participant.

At the briefing
▪ Frame the issue for maximum impact and significance.
▪ Communicate the key messages.
▪ Brief media on specific legislative or electoral measures, but do not give away strategic or confidential information. You do not want your opponents to read about your strategy in the paper!
▪ Limit yourself to no more than four minutes per person. Suggest story ideas as you speak. Reinforce key messages.
▪ Provide updates on news: "Since you last reported on this issue…"
▪ Walk through a clear, brief overview of the main issues and your position.
▪ Pitch story ideas.
▪ Educate media about anticipated tactics and rhetoric of opposition.
▪ Anticipate questions from reporters.
▪ Often stories will not come exclusively from the briefing; then again, they might. Your work in educating the reporters will pay off later as they cover the issue. But remember, everything said during the briefing is typically considered to be "on the record" and can be used in a story.
▪ Thank everyone for attending. If you made promises during the meeting—"We can deliver the report to you ahead of time" or "If you want to talk to the community person beforehand, we can make that happen"—follow up and deliver on the promise. After the briefing, send out thank you notes.

Case study

The editorial board review

The following example shows how one organization turned around a history of hostile coverage and negative editorializing by conducting an editorial board review with the local paper. Reviews can also be used to pitch op eds or get a paper to take and editorial stand.

Who we are

Environmental Health Coalition (EHC) is an environmental justice and toxics cleanup organization founded in 1980. Working with communities in the San Diego/Tijuana region, EHC is dedicated to the prevention and cleanup of toxic pollution threatening our health, our communities and the environment. We promote environmental justice, monitor government and industry actions that cause pollution, educate communities about toxic hazards and toxics-use reduction and empower the public to join our cause.

Diane Takvorian
Executive Director
Environmental Health Coalition
1717 Kettner Blvd., Ste. 100
San Diego, CA 92101
(P) 619 235-0281
(F) 619 232-3670
(E) tracig@environmentalhealth.org
www.environmentalhealth.org

EHC is one of only a small number of progressive organizations in politically conservative San Diego. We have fought for public health and environmental justice for nearly twenty years. EHC has been forced to do battle on multiple fronts: forcing cleanup of contaminated sites, fighting for zoning laws that separate residential areas from polluting industries, organizing opposition to toxic waste incinerators, preserving the fragile ecosystem of San Diego Bay and holding U.S. companies accountable for their operations in Mexico.

San Diego Union-Tribune—bastion of conservatism

There is one major daily newspaper in San Diego, the *San Diego Union-Tribune* (SDUT). As you might guess, its editorial perspective has historically been quite conservative. Challenging the corporate and government institutions in San Diego made EHC the target of the SDUT's editorials on many occasions. Our regular response to these editorials had been to organize our allies to send letters refuting the frequent misstatements and to submit a letter to the editor from the organization.

In 1997, after working with the SPIN Project to develop a more proactive media strategy, we decided to address the situation with the SDUT editorial board head-on. Our objectives were to:
• Challenge the SDUT's misrepresentation of EHC's positions on environmental health and justice issues.
• Point out the inaccuracies in previous editorials.
• Demonstrate the credibility of EHC leadership and competence on our key issues.
• Provide an overview of the key issues with which we are concerned.
• Negotiate an agreement that SDUT would contact EHC prior to running editorials about our work or issues.

What we did

Meeting with the editorial board of a major metropolitan newspaper is a big deal. Local movers and shakers have pretty good access to the paper and appear to be regular visitors. Grassroots folks, on the other hand, either do not ask to meet with them or are denied access. The board is comprised of all of the paper's editors and some include reporters as well. To prepare for our meeting we:
• Wrote a letter to the editor of the editorial page requesting a meeting. The letter provided a brief summary of our concerns and the rationale for the meeting.
• Compiled all of the editorials that mentioned EHC, our responses and other letters to the editor.
• Researched and compiled other editorials on environmental issues.

• Researched and compiled editorials on other controversial and high-profile individuals and organizations.

The newspapers have made research much easier with the Internet. We were able to search the editorial pages and news articles separately for various topics, individuals and organizations in a relatively short period of time. Our research revealed that:

• The SDUT had written 11 editorials in six years directly criticizing and maligning EHC.

• No other organization or individual had been criticized as often as EHC, and most were not even mentioned as often—including the mayor!

• There were repeated and blatant factual errors in every editorial.

• There had never been any communication between the editorial writers and EHC staff prior to the publication of any of the 11 editorials.

• The SDUT had taken positions on some issues identical to those of EHC, but never credited us.

We compiled all of the documents and analysis into a tabbed briefing book for easy reference. We organized a committee consisting of three of our board members and the executive director to represent EHC to the editorial board. Prior to the scheduled meeting we met with our board to review the research and analysis, prepare our presentation and assign roles and functions to each participant.

The meeting

Seven representatives of the SDUT editorial board were present at the meeting: the editor of the Editorial Page, two editorial writers, the editor of the Opinion/Editorial Page, the Letters editor and two environmental reporters.

Key aspects of the meeting for us were

• A presentation of EHC's concerns based on our research. We quickly responded to the editor's assumption that our objective was to convince them to adopt our position on issues to which they were firmly opposed. We made it clear that we wanted to be heard on all issues and that we expected to be on opposite sides—*some* of the time. Our major assertion was that we were not on opposite sides all of the time.

• Identification of the editorial writer with the grudge against EHC. We knew who was writing most of the editorials and had specifically requested that he be in attendance. He quickly revealed that in addition to being the author of the editorials, he was also very uninformed of the issues about which he was writing.

• Isolation of the editorial writer from his peers. EHC representatives were very disciplined about our presentation and responded to the problem editorial writer. Our data notebook allowed us to quickly refute his inaccurate assertions about various topics. Therefore, the other editors and reporters quickly understood that they were all on shaky ground. We had also worked extensively with both reporters on news stories; they supported our factual assertions and expressed dismay at the editorial writer's lack of research.

• Healthy debate with the editorial board. We selected a couple of upcoming topics and briefly presented them to the board as important emerging issues. A vigorous discussion ensued about each, demonstrating our credibility and critical thinking.

• Agreement to talk. We ended the meeting with several points of agreement including: any editorial writer commenting on our position in the future would first call us to check facts; EHC would send our news releases to the editors and reporters— something we had never done before; we would continue to communicate informally about emerging issues.

After the meeting, where we are now

The process of preparing for and meeting with the editorial board was a positive one from many perspectives:

• The organization felt empowered by taking a proactive stance.

• The research and analysis allowed us to take a more objective, long-term view of the situation, and develop an effective strategy.

• We formed positive relationships with the other editors and have placed opinion editorial pieces and letters to the editor with much more frequency.

• Dialogue with the editorial page editor is now open and constructive.

• No editorials maligning EHC have run in the year since our meeting.

Overall, the most important benefit of the strategy was opening the eyes of the editorial board to the credibility of EHC's positions. While they have taken positions in opposition to our views, they are now more factual and appear to be less reactionary. Amazingly, they have even taken positions in agreement with those of EHC, but have yet to credit us with "being right." Oh well, maybe next year.

—Diane Takvorian

Staging media events

Sooner or later, if your voice is going to be heard proactively in the media debate, you have to make news. That means staging a media event, among other things. This section offers tips, case studies and checklists for capturing media attention at successful media events.

Press conferences vs. media events

There are "press conferences" and there are "media events." In our experience, reporters prefer "media events" to "press conferences." It is more than a simple semantic difference.

Press conferences are typically characterized by highly controlled, formalized settings featuring official speakers delivering scripted comments, with a Q&A session following, all usually held indoors in an office-like space or briefing room. They often are called to respond to some news development, such as releasing a statement, or they make news themselves, such as releasing a report or making a newsworthy announcement.

Media events usually feature more spontaneity and contain an element of staging, drama, color, action and surprise. While press conferences can present a visual image, media events usually feature more photo opportunities and hence are more attractive to television. Media events are, well, events. They feature groups of people doing something visually interesting that symbolizes or evokes your message, as well as decorations and speakers. They are often held outdoors.

What to hold—a press conference or full-blown media event—depends on the nature of your news and the appropriate venue for it. The pros of press conferences are: (a) easier to manage and control information and message, and keep track of reporters; (b) more professional and serious; (c) convenience of location. The cons of press conferences are: (a) too managed, too serious, too professional; and (b) reporters resist being kept track of, and instead prefer the spontaneity of roaming around to find new angles on a story. Media events are more visual, spontaneous and dramatic, but harder to manage the many elements and control the message.

The challenge is to find a way to dramatize and visualize your news to make it more interesting and appealing to television in particular. Instead of simply releasing statistics or a statement, organize a rally, vigil, protest or street theater action that drives home your messages.

More tips for media events

1 Be mindful of diversity in terms of speakers at your press conference or media event. Strive for a rich representation, including people of color, age and gender diversity, as well as "types" of people (officials and regular folk). The idea of conducting a press conference that features a line up of five white straight men is almost impossible to imagine at this point. Speaking at an official news event is an honor and carries with it community importance and personal significance. Use your position as a media activist to ensure that those rarely represented in the media are in fact featured at your media events.

2 Decorate tastefully and appropriately. Create attention-getting visuals at your media event that emphasize the visual story. For outdoor media events, this could include banners, signage and other large-scale decorative elements. For indoor press conferences, consider charts, graphs or blow-up photos and other graphics. Do not forget to put a copy of your group's logo on the front of the podium where cameras can see it. Put something on the wall behind you, a banner or a sign, for example, that contains your message in a couple of key words or graphics.

A word of caution: Do not go overboard in decorating your event to the point reporters cannot find the news through all the bric-a-brac.

3 If you are releasing a report or other document, hold the document up beside your head at the podium for several seconds while you are speaking about it ("As this report shows for the first time…") This gives photographers an opportunity to take the picture. It may feel awkward, like you are the product showcase girl on the "Price

Boredom: The enemy of news events

Media events come in many different forms—from huge marches and rallies to modest but poignant vigils. From newsbreaking press conferences to fabulous photo ops. Whatever event or press conference you decide to do, the key is: Do not bore the media. Make your event exciting, visually engaging and newsworthy. Your chances of attracting reporters will be much better.

In his tell-it-like-it-is book, *Making the News, A Guide for nonprofits and Activists* (Westview Press, 1998), media activist Jason Salzman writes: "Successful media events are, above all else, entertaining. That doesn't mean amusing. In fact, some successful media events are somewhat disgusting. But whether amusing or disgusting—they are engaging, and that is the key synonym for entertainment in the media."

So resist the temptation to sponsor another boring affair that disinterests reporters. Instead, invest your news with creative flair and dynamic presentation that attracts reporters to your story.

Staging media events and press conferences

Hold them only when you have news. Reporters dread news events in which no news is made. Do not waste reporters' time with non-events, or events designed simply to promote your name. Actually make news (new announcement, new report released, protest staged, etc.) at your event.

Decide if you need a media event or not. Perhaps you do not need a full-blown media event to make news. Depending on your story, a well-placed pitch phone call to a reporter, resulting in a feature article, may suffice. Or place an opinion editorial. Media events are labor intensive and costly so conduct them sparingly. Sponsor too many events and reporters will "cry wolf" and be skeptical of your intentions.

Determine who the news is for. Before you make news at your event you must target your audience. The audience for your news will determine what kind of event you stage and what media is invited. That means where you stage the event, who speaks, what the banners look like and numerous other details will be colored by your target audience. For example, events promoting youth-related messages will look and sound very different from other kinds of events, and will be designed to attract media that serves young people.

Good and bad news days. Schedule your event with the best timing in mind. Do not stage your events late in the afternoon or evening when many reporters are on deadline. Mondays are not preferred because offices will be closed over the previous weekend and you may not be able to reach key reporters for a couple of days before the event. Fridays are not so good either because the news may come out in Saturday's media—the least read issue of the newspaper and the day everyone is at the beach or working in the yard.

Good time for media events. Late morning for press conferences is a good time; lunch hour if you are trying to attract participants to a rally; and midweek is good when other news may be slow. Of course, you can never really predict slow news days. And the reality of your organizing may dictate other times. If you must stage a rally after work, for example, at least do it during the evening television news so the stations can send cameras

---

is Right," but do it for the photo.

4 Spin and schmooze reporters. Your media event is your time to shine, so personally greet each reporter, make sure they have statements and press kits, give them your business card or contact number, ensure they are comfortable and taken care of, be a resource for them in terms of securing interviews and other information and keep spinning the message to them. "Did you hear so-and-so speak?" one media activist could be heard asking a reporter. "I thought her message about so-and-so was so strong and key." This activist obviously is spinning the message to the reporter following the event to make sure it was heard.

5 Hold questions to the end of the press conference. Take questions one at a time and either have the key host answer them or pass the question to another speaker.

When you are finished, end the press conference and thank reporters for coming. Do not dally or speak off the cuff to fill time—for you may say something you wish you had not.

6 Do your follow-up. After the event or press conference is not the time to relax even though you may be exhausted. Keep the adrenaline running for a few more hours. First, check the reporter sign-in list to see who showed up and who did not. Call the no-shows and offer to courier over a press kit and pitch the story again. For key reporters who did show, a follow-up call to check in with them back at the office may be appreciated. Do not abandon your office phone or cellular. Stay close to a phone while reporters are writing the story on deadline because they may need an extra quote or to check a fact.

for live coverage. If held on the weekend, make sure both key reporters who normally work during the week and the weekend crew know about the event.

Avoid being "bumped." Check for competing events. Beware of scheduling your news event on days when other major news will be made. For example, if the Pope or the President is coming to your town, do not pick that day to make news unrelated to their visits. Same goes for days when major local events will dominate coverage, such as big civic parades or sporting spectacles. Your news event most likely will be bumped off the pages and airwaves because of the competition for reporters' time. Check community contacts, calendars or what else is happening that day. Call around to other groups to see if they have anything scheduled.

Keep the event short. About 30 to 45 minutes is the length of a good media event, especially press conferences. Major rallies of course may go on longer but reporters will get their stories soon enough after the first few speakers and then head back to the news room. At the SPIN Project we like press conferences that are tight, informative and well constructed.

Rallies and marches. If your event is a major, all-day rally, march or similar gathering, stack the first three speakers with your key spokespersons and instruct them to communicate the messages from the stage. In fact, the very first speaker—besides being the welcoming "host"—should communicate the key messages in his or her speech. After the first few speakers, reporters may tend to drift away to interview other people. The rest of the speaker line-up may or may not be heard by reporters, but at least the messages were communicated at the beginning when attention was highest.

Location. Location. Location. Make your event convenient to reporters, yet dynamic and appropriate in terms of backdrop. Do not make a pack of reporters travel hundreds or even dozens of miles to get the story. Bring the story to them if you have to. The further away from their newsrooms, the more reluctant they will be to cover it unless the event is earth-shattering in importance. Keep the event close to them and you will make their lives easier.

If you must bring the story to reporters, symbolize the location. For example, if you are celebrating the clean-up of a river following your environmental conservation campaign but the river is too far away, then bring the river to town. Fill up clear jugs of river water, or pools in which kids can play, or a pyramid of glasses containing free samples of drinking water, and stage a photo op downtown.

Make the location appropriate to the issue. The backdrop should symbolize and frame the news, not distract from it.

Check reporters in and rope off media areas. Have reporters sign in at a check-in table at both press conferences and media events. Hand them press kits and schmooze them. Some press conferences may offer coffee or other refreshments to reporters. Do not offer anything lavish. For big outdoor rally-type media events, inform reporters in advance in the media advisory the location of the press area—typically near the stage or the command center. Hang a big sign nearby that says MEDIA. At big

Example

Your Family, Friends and Neighbors, a gay rights group in Idaho, co-sponsored a media event in front of the historic Freedom Bell on the steps of the state capitol in Boise. The event was to announce their campaign to defeat a controversial anti-gay ballot measure that would have permitted discrimination based on sexual orientation. These activists linked their campaign to Idaho's legacy of freedom and framed it as a justice and equality issue. Meanwhile, the group sponsoring the homophobic measure, an Idaho arch-conservative "family values" group, chose the public bathroom in the local park as their background, claiming "actual homosexuals" had sex there and that is why the ballot measure should be passed. These activists linked their campaign to stereotypes of gay people and framed it as "perversion." Both backdrops obviously framed the news in unique ways. The anti-gay ballot measure was defeated and Your Family, Friends and Neighbors won.

events, section off a media chill-out area (affectionately called bull pens), where reporters can conduct interviews, rendezvous with sources and generally hang out. The media chill area is a good place to have water and other refreshments and a cell phone. Control access to this area. Run your featured speakers through this area for media "availabilities" and one-on-one interviews.

Set your speakers lineup

Limit your key speakers at press conferences to three or four maximum. The first speaker welcomes, hosts, introduces other speakers and communicates the key messages. Other speakers echo the message and add depth. At bigger outdoor media events, the first one or two speakers are key and definitely should speak before others, including performers or entertainers. If you have the lineup set, publicize it to reporters in a media advisory. Hand out a list of speakers with short bios for each.

Typical speakers might include

■ an executive director or other key staff person, board member or designated spokesperson of your organization;
■ a person or two representing the personal human interest (e.g., your "poster child");
■ a public official, celebrity, local politician or ally;
■ an "expert," say, the author of the report you are releasing or the lawyer in charge of a case.

If a politician is invited, they must be allowed to speak out of proper protocol (when do politicians ever pass an opportunity to speak?!), but usually they are not first in the lineup. Your staff person who is handling media may open the press conference by making housekeeping announcements such as "pick up your press kits" or "we will start in five minutes" or "hold questions to the end," and then turn it over to the main speaker/host.

Five minutes maximum for each speaker is fine.

A note about the "Geraldo Row": Got too many "experts" who want to be visible at your press conference, including every ally in your coalition, and afraid to hurt their feelings by saying no? Obviously they cannot all speak, otherwise you will be there all day (and reporters will leave). Feature your VIPs off to the side or arrayed behind the podium in a row of distinguished experts—otherwise known as the Geraldo Row after the talk show format of having key guests on stage and secondary speakers off stage. These folks are introduced and offered for interviews and statements after the press conference, but do not speak individually. Their statements may be included in the press kit.

Practice your event. For press conferences, consider a "dress rehearsal" the day before with your speakers (at least those who can attend). Fire questions that reporters may ask at the speakers during the rehearsal, and test any audio visual equipment you may be using.

Checklist for news events

✔ News defined?
✔ Audience targeted?
✔ Messages honed (talking points scripted)?
✔ Location, time and date scheduled?
✔ Room confirmed for press conference? Space for media event?
✔ Calendar checked for conflicts?
✔ Speakers identified and confirmed?
✔ Media advisory drafted and sent to reporters?
✔ Deliverables produced (press kit, reports, videos, etc.)?
✔ Logistics team in place for media event (security, crew, volunteers, etc.)
✔ Decorations produced (banners, posters, podium logo, charts, etc.)
✔ Pitch calls to reporters made?
✔ Dress rehearsal for speakers at press conference?
✔ AV equipment secured for space?
✔ Refreshments confirmed (if ordered)?

At the press conference or media event:
✔ "Bull pen" media area roped off?
✔ Press kits stuffed and ready to be handed out? Signage put up?
✔ Media check-in sheet put out? Someone assigned to staff the check-in desk at all times?
✔ Speakers show up?
✔ Props and decorations in place?
✔ Reporters greeted and checked in as they arrive?
✔ First speaker starts on time (within 5 minutes of scheduled time)?
✔ Other speakers on time?
✔ Q&A period starts?
✔ Follow-up spin after Q&A?
✔ Follow-up work completed (no-shows contacted)?

63

Photo opportunities

They say a picture speaks a thousand words. In the media, a picture speaks a million soundbites. For good or for bad, one strong, well-staged photograph can communicate volumes and move messages faster than a dozen press conferences. Welcome to the world of photo ops.

The much-maligned photo op is often abused and misused. There are too many sparkling-teeth celebrities "giving face," and grip-and-grin politicians with big hair. We need to reclaim the photo op and make it ours!

Tips for better photo ops

First and foremost, always find ways to visualize your news. Here is the blunt reality of how it works: No picture, no image. No image, no television, no photographers. No television, no thousands, if not millions, of audience members seeing your message. Television in particular needs pictures. So instead of just presenting talking heads in suits, behind podiums, beneath bad fluorescent lights, in boring office suites, create photo ops for your news. Even press conferences are occasionally covered on television. So remember to keep this in mind when setting one up.

Stage the photo op with the message in mind

Visualize how everything will come together and look in tonight's TV news or tomorrow's paper. How will the viewer get the one key message that drives home your point? Find the one visual metaphor that communicates the message.

Do not overload the picture with too much visual data

You risk confusing the message. Some photo ops have so much going on—banners, flags, ribbons, posters, charts, people, pets, politicians, props—that it is difficult to discern what the event is about. Do not go overboard and turn your news into an inappropriate three-ring spectacle. The messages should be enhanced by the photo op, not obscured. And remember, if it is too gimmicky, you may get a backlash from reporters.

Media event or press conference—what is the better photo op?

An important consideration is whether to stage a *media event* or a *press conference*. Press conferences, usually reserved for auspicious and official-looking news making, are often dreaded by reporters. They tend to be boring and long. On the other hand, press conferences allow you to control as much of the message as possible. Media events can be much more exciting and feature photo ops, protests, rallies, speak outs or town halls. Unfortunately, public media events are more difficult to control and can get sloppy if not carefully managed. But on the whole, highly visual and galvanizing media events are superior to press conferences in terms of both interest and impact.

Make correct spelling a priority

Photographers and camera crews should have the correct spelling of the names of people in the picture, if possible. This is obviously not necessary for crowd shots. They should also get a press kit or press release explaining the action.

Be mindful of camera angles and the direction of the sun

Lighting at outdoor events matters significantly. Do not make camera people shoot directly into the sun. Also, does the backdrop "read" in your picture? In other words, can you make sense of it? One hapless group in Washington, D.C. staged their photo op right at the base of the Washington Monument. All you could see was some marble thing behind them. The inspiring structure they had desired was out of the picture because they were too close!

Slow down

If you know a camera crew is on the way or you can see a photographer running to catch your action, slow down. Give them time to set up and get the picture. Do not hesitate to stop the action or slow it down so cameras get the best image. Shameless manipulators of a dramatic picture? You bet!

Let press know about "media visuals"

Include a note about media visuals at the end of your media advisories that informs reporters what images to expect.

Example:

The Environmental Health Coalition (EHC) was involved in a years-long campaign to get the San Diego Port Authority to ban the use of toxic spraying in the poor Barrio Logan neighborhood. A local fumigation company sprayed fruit with the toxic agent, which endangered the health of local residents, most of them Latinos. EHC organized a dramatic rally and march through the neighborhood, culminating at the fence of the fumigation plant. Banners and signs were multi-lingual for Spanish and English language media. There, residents of the neighborhood tied blue and white ribbons to the fence to symbolize the clean air they needed to breathe. Meanwhile, more residents protested the actual meeting of the Port Authority, pressuring its members to vote to stop the fumigation. There, more ribbons were handed out. Upon winning the vote, the children of the neighborhood presented the officials with ribbons. Local television and print media captured the photo op, which drove home the message that empowered neighborhood residents were dynamically involved in improving the health and well-being of their community.

Making news with your report

Releasing a report or study can be a good opportunity to attract the media to your issue, providing there actually is news to be revealed. Reports analyze issues, provide information and facts, expose controversy, contextualize issues into broader political and social arenas, chart trends and give voice to those affected. Besides being organizing and public educational tools, reports themselves can make news, especially when combined with media events that "visualize" or depict the findings.

There are specific ways to construct a report and release it to the media so your message is communicated most effectively. The following are tips for making news with reports:

Framing the report

First and foremost, the report should be easy to read and factually accurate. All data should be corroborated and confirmed. The larger mainstream media outlets will often have fact checkers peruse the report for statistical accuracy.

The report should conform to statistical and journalistic accuracy, but will obviously reflect your spin. The goal of the report is to draw attention to the issue, frame it for maximum media and political impact, move your messages and influence policy. Balance the statistical portion of the report—which can be dry and numerical—with aggressive, hard-hitting language that summarizes your findings and communicates your messages, and with dramatic human interest stories.

Your report should advocate and educate. Not only will community activists read it, but elected officials, policy-makers and reporters might too. In fact, at the SPIN Project we believe the main audience for a hard-hitting report should be reporters and news-makers. We counsel activists to prepare the report with this audience in mind. The tone of the report must communicate academic integrity while maintaining a strong point of view.

From the very beginning of the report, in both its conceptualization and execution, design it to frame the issue and create political or cultural change.

If the report is the first of its kind, say so. Call it "unprecedented," "new" or "groundbreaking."

Start with the title. Think about calling it something provocative and attention-getting. Use a tag that frames the issue right from the beginning.

Keep it short. Long, thousand-page tomes will not be read by most reporters. A 40 to 50 page document, including the appendix, is a good read.

Here is a useful guide to structuring your report so it is easy for reporters to read:

Cover

Should contain title, tag line and name of the report's sponsor.

Table of contents

Clearly annotated for ease of reading and finding separate sections.

Executive summary

This section should read like a press release. It is the first thing reporters will see and sometimes the only thing they will read. The executive summary will frame the issue, summarize the news, move your strategic key messages, present key findings and provide the most important facts. It must be concise, rarely longer than two or three pages. The key thing about the executive summary is that it will *conclude* something. It can conclude anything you want it to conclude as long as you can back up the conclusion with your data and evidence. The *conclusion* is your frame, your message, your advocacy.

Overview section

This is the main body of the report. It typically contains: an elaboration on the findings; more in-depth facts and analysis; historical, legal and political contextualization; and a small, "greatest hits" sampling of personal testimonials.

Methodology section

This provides all the logistical and statistical background on how you did the report. This will bolster the factual integrity of your work. Include this section in the overview or right before it.

"Profiles"

Also known as personal testimonials or a listing of incidents. This often is the most dramatic section as it highlights the impact of the issue on real people.

Example: In the previously cited gay-bashing report, the "incidents" section was subdivided—murder, physical assaults, vandalism—and included graphic descriptions of the attacks along with words from the victims. A grueling read for any person, but an effective way to document the incidents and put a human face on them.

Action or recommendations

This section concludes the main body of the report. This is where you reiterate any calls for action you have made in the executive summary and lay out the policy decisions needed to fix the problem.

Appendix

This closes the report. It usually includes charts, tables, graphs, press clips and other information.

Graphics

Consider having your report designed and professionally produced without going overboard. Why spend all that time and money only to produce a dreary document that poorly reflects the professionalism of your group? In addition to charts and other graphic items, photographs and illustrations can drive home the points made in your report. As we said, just do not go overboard. We have seen reports that looked like postmodern avant-garde design competition entries in which the news was way too difficult to find amid all the typefaces, ding-bats and other graphic goo-gaws. On the other hand, we have also seen sleep-inducing documents featuring page after gray page of type with no break.

Releasing the report

Do not let the beautiful report you produce collect dust. You need an aggressive, proactive media plan to communicate the report's messages. Key points to consider when planning for your media are:

Pick the appropriate strategy for making news

Some reports may require a more low-key approach, such as placing a story on the report by briefing one or two cultivated reporters. Other reports deserve the full media spin treatment, such as press events, rallies, photo ops—the works.

Determine the "scope" of the news

Is your news national in scope with local tie-ins, or local in scope with national implications? Along with your budget and resources, this will determine what kind of media effort to unleash.

Embargoes and your report

You will often provide an advance copy of your report to key reporters. This allows them to familiarize themselves with the data and do a better, more in-depth job of writing the story. The moment you give reporters the news, they can technically run with it—unless you embargo it. To embargo your news means to place a restriction on when the story can run—"EMBARGOED UNTIL WEDNESDAY, OCT. 21, 10 A.M." Print in big letters on the cover and on all related materials.

Reporters typically do not break embargoes. If a reporter does break the embargo, be prepared to: respond and voice your disappointment; assuage other reporters that the leak was not your fault; and move on and ride the story now that it is out of the gate—unless it can be contained.

If you live in a two-paper town—one with morning and afternoon editions—be mindful that a morning embargo may eliminate the morning newspaper and allow the afternoon paper to get the story first.

For those making coast-to-coast news, remember to take time zones into account when setting the time for your embargo release. Also remember that radio, the fastest media after the Internet, can run with a story the moment the calendar turns to the date of the embargo—if there is no specified time embargo. And speaking of the Internet, some online media will run a story almost instantaneously.

If the report is national in nature, consider one national media event focal point—usually in Washington, D.C.—in coordination with local media events. If the report is local in nature, emphasize the national implications of the findings in terms of how other states or communities deal with the issue and how your report affects the national debate.

Placing the report with a key journalist

Should you decide on the more subtle, strategic approach of placing the report to key journalists, you will most likely do so through a media briefing with the reporter or a collection of reporters and editors (*see "Organizing successful media briefings and editorial board reviews," page 56*).

Sometimes you can do both: "leak" the news to one key reporter, and soon after (one or two days), hold a media event to release it to everyone else. This is not entirely deceptive and is commonly done. Some news-making reports are given to a key media reporter who does an advance on it that comes out either the day of or the day before your media event. This can fuel coverage of the news by other reporters. This is called "pack journalism," when reporters rush together for a hot news story for fear of being left out. Of course, be aware that you cannot control exactly when, where or how the story will come out with the original reporter, so there is some risk involved.

The full-on media campaign

If you decide on a full-fledged, multi-component media campaign to release your report, consider these steps:

1. Produce a media kit that contains the report, your press release, supportive fact sheets and other materials (*see "The press kit," page 48*).
2. Stage an attention-getting media event that visualizes the news. This can be a press conference featuring key staff people, the author, leading politicians, plus personal "testifiers." Release the report accompanied by a photo op: a rally, protest or some other event. Give the media—in particular television—something to tape or photograph.

The point is, do not release your report in some boring room. **Stage** the news when you release the report and give reporters a dramatic media **event** to punctuate it.

■ Why stop with just the media event? Go all the way with your **media plan**.

■ Conduct **media briefings** before the report is released to make sure key reporters are prepped and have access to the key facts and players, including the author(s).

■ Write and place an **opinion editorial** timed to come out on or close to the day you release the report (*see "Opinion editorials and letters to the editor," page 71*).

■ Pitch the story to radio and TV; book yourself on local **talk shows**.

■ Once the story has broken, send in the **letters to the editor** to keep it alive for a few more days.

■ Track coverage and gather clips of articles.

Releasing a report

The following example offers a good model for constructing and releasing a news-making report.

Cathi Tactaquin
Executive Director
National Network for Immigrant and Refugee Rights
310 8th St., Ste. 307
Oakland, CA 94607
(P) 510 465-1984
(F) 510 465-1885
(E) nnirr@nnirr.org
www.nnirr.org

Raids conducted by the U.S. Immigration and Naturalization Service (INS) are a huge problem in America, especially as immigrants continue to be made into scapegoats for the problems of the nation. The INS targets suspected havens—including those in white, middle- and upper-middle-class communities—of so-called "illegal immigrants." The raids are extremely disruptive, often violent and horribly dehumanizing. The victims—most of them people of color—are then deported. Too often families are torn apart and communities shredded. Occasionally, legally documented citizens are swept up in the raids. Latinos in particular are targeted for this abuse. The National Network for Immigrant and Refugee Rights (NNIRR) and the National INS Raids Task Force produced an unprecedented, groundbreaking report on the increased incidence of raids and their disastrous impacts.

The Title: "Portrait of Injustice: The Impact of Immigration Raids on Families, Workers and Communities."

The Report contained 63 pages divided into six key sections:
• Executive Summary;
• Overview—including three subsections: About This Report; Historical, Political and Legislative Context for INS Raids; Methodology;
• Principal Findings;
• Profiles—divided into three subsections: Individual Impact, Community Impact, Other Incidents of Abuse;
• Recommendations;
• Appendix.

A "Table of Contents" preceded the main section of the report, but followed the "Executive Summary" and a special "Key Findings" break-out section. This layout allowed reporters to get the news and messages as soon as they opened the cover.

The Frame and the Message: The first two sentences of the opening paragraph of the first section in the "Executive Summary" spelled out the news, framed it for maximum impact, and moved the message:

"Portrait of Injustice" finds that immigration raids are pervasive in communities across the U.S. and have a devastating impact on workplaces, neighborhoods and community institutions. Based on an examination of 235 raids around the country, this groundbreaking report concludes that raids threaten the rights of citizens and non-citizens—violating constitutional protections, destabilizing families and undermining workers' rights.

The rest of the report reinforced this frame and communicated the message that the raids must stop. Note how the buzzwords—"pervasive," "across the U.S.," "devastating," "groundbreaking," "threaten the rights of citizens and non-citizens"—communicate a sense of urgency and national/local impact. In other words: Frame the issue for maximum impact.

The Look: The report is a handsome, professionally designed, nicely laid-out document that communicates a sense of research integrity and human empathy. It looks rich in both information and drama without being expensive or flashy. Dramatic and captioned black-and-white photos of actual victims of raids bring home

Report covers can dramatize and frame the issue.

69

Continued on next page

the issue's impact. The cover features a poignant full-page photo of a woman and her daughter. (The mother actually gave birth while her husband was put on a bus to be deported to Mexico following a raid at a poultry plant in Oregon!) Convenient "sidebars," subsections, useful checklists and a raids monitoring form are interspersed throughout the document. Plenty of white space remains within the report, making it easy to read despite the abundance of data.

The Plan: The National Network conducted an ambitious grassroots organizing, education, training and media release plan for the report. Several weeks before the report was finished they organized a conference to bring together key community activists, brief them on the report, get their input for the plan, find hooks for the release in their local communities, and get them on message. The SPIN Project conducted a media training at this event.

In advance of the release, NNIRR produced the press kit, created a targeted media list—national and local—and distributed a "Media Organizing Kit"

to dozens of communities nationwide. The Media Organizing Kit contained:

- A "message page"—talking points.
- Suggested local events—rallies, vigils, speakouts, etc.—to create photo ops with local spin.
- Standardized press releases, letters to the editors, media advisories, and other materials.

Key reporters were already given copies of the actual report—embargoed until the official release date (see "Embargoes and your report," page 67).

The report was released at a press conference in Washington, D.C. in conjunction with scores of local media events staged at numerous locations across the country. The news hit media in several cities at the same time as the national press picked up the D.C. event. The NNIRR's thorough planning resulted in the story "crisscrossing the news wires"—scoring both national and local coverage. In addition, the story had "legs." Follow-up features and profiles kept the news alive for days and weeks after the event.

—Cathi Tactaquin

Research is key for making news

Leon Sompolinsky

Preparation is essential to any well-orchestrated media relations campaign. And research is the key. There are many ways to conduct research. For your news to have power and influence, the authors of your reports and documents will be keen on producing the most statistically correct, hard-hitting, strategic manuscripts possible—no matter what method is used.

One service of tremendous use to community activists is the DataCenter, based in Oakland, CA. Using online information to access thousands of newspapers, journals and magazines simultaneously, the DataCenter's ImpactResearch Team (DIRT) has assisted the media campaigns of numerous grassroots groups and media organizations. Current and past clients include: the Environmental Health Coalition, ACORN, Communities for a Better Environment, We Interrupt This Message and the Public Media Center.

Leon Sompolinsky
Information Activist
Data Center
1904 Franklin St., Suite 900
Oakland, CA 94612-2912
(P) 510 835-4699
(F) 510 835-3017
(E) datacenter@datacenter.org
www.igc.org/datacenter

Here are some examples of what targeted research has enabled organizations to do:

- With our assistance, the Political Ecology Group successfully prevented the Sierra Club from adopting a divisive policy on immigration by tracking press coverage and exposing the racist background and right-wing connections of the organizations

pressuring the Sierra Club to vote on this issue.

- The Western States Center analyzed and countered the sudden appearance in the corporate press of the term "eco-terrorism" closely associated with reports on the Unabomber.
- The Center for Commercial Free Public Education wrote a report and held a press conference to publicize the corporate support of attacks on high school environmental curriculum.
- Political Research Associates reviewed past press reporting to identify journalists' interests in pitching a critical story about the "Promise Keepers" to coincide with an East Coast revival.

These are some of the ways research can inform *your* media relations campaign:

- Identify reporters covering your issue.
- Provide examples of a reporters' work to understand their style and interests.
- Identify trends.
- Track media coverage.
- Follow stories to correct inaccurate or misleading reporting.
- Respond to quickly breaking news stories connected to your issue.
- Identify and monitor real and potential friends and foes.

The media is always on the lookout for good copy. Research can help you pitch your story and shape the news.

Opinion editorials and letters to the editor

You can use the media to communicate your message directly to your audiences without relying on reporters to write stories. This can be done with opinion editorials and letters to the editor.

Op eds, as opinion editorials are called, are often an underused weapon in a media arsenal—yet frequently they constitute the most popular part of the newspaper. Op eds give you an opportunity to move your messages in your own voice, in essay form and in a way that captivates and galvanizes audiences.

Letters to the editor, while often "reactive" to news already reported, can keep the story alive and the debate raging. Journalism is one of the rare professions in which controversy is good. Reporters get "extra points" when their stories spark debate. A furious "letters war" on the letters-to-the-editor page warms the hearts of reporters and delights editors. Among other things, it means people are reading the paper. But for you, these letters give your news "legs": The story keeps running long after the initial media event was covered.

Note: Op eds and letters to the editor are different than "editorials." Editorials are positions the media takes on particular issues. They are generated by the editorial department of the media outlet. You may influence the media outlet's position and urge it to editorialize on an issue (*see "Organizing successful media briefings and editorial board reviews," page 56*), but you never write the editorial. You write the op ed or letter to the editor. There are also "advertorials"—marketing pitches cleverly disguised as editorials by companies selling something—and "infomercials"—sales pitches disguised as news articles. Advertisers will pay for these pieces. Op eds and letters are free.

Tip
Opinion editorials

Make them personal, not academic.

Determine who is the best "voice" for the op ed. Is it your executive director? Notable community leader? Community spokesperson personally affected by the issue? Local or national celebrity?

Write concisely: Five hundred to 800 words will usually do the trick. Check op ed length restrictions in your local paper. Use short sentences and short paragraphs—usually no more than three short sentences per paragraph.

Compose a captivating lead paragraph to catch readers' attention.

Frame the issue within the first three paragraphs.

Communicate your messages soon after framing the issue. One entire paragraph should be just your messages. Repeat your messages at the end.

Elaborate on your points and always keep the reader engaged. Among other things, do not go on tangents that load the piece with technical jargon.

Cite compelling examples or heart-tugging anecdotes to reinforce your position. If humor works, use it.

Make the op ed timely. Do not write about something that is old news or off the media radar screen.

Pitch the op ed to the opinion editorial or editorial page editor. Call first to gauge the interest; then fax it over with a cover letter. Follow up to make sure the fax went through and ask if the paper is going to run it. Do not submit the op ed to competing media. Go with your best shot first; if that does not work, try another media outlet or rewrite it.

Make certain the editor has your contact name and number.

Aim for running the op ed as close as possible to your news event. If you get the paper to run the op ed on the day of your big press conference, a big gold star to you!

Placing an op ed

Writing an opinion editorial is one way to bring prominence to your issue. However, the writing is the easy part. Placing an op ed takes a lot of pitching, especially if a paper has been hostile to your side of the story *(see "Organizing successful media briefings and editorial board reviews," page 56)*.

The following example comes from David Bacon, a freelance journalist and board member of the Northern California Coalition for Immigrant Rights (NCCIR). As part of a national week of action launched by NCCIR's parent organization, National Network for Immigrant and Refugee Rights (NNIRR), NCCIR wanted to respond to the lack of fair coverage of immigrants' rights in a mainstream newspaper in San Francisco.

Prior to the appearance of this op ed, a major San Francisco daily newspaper had published a series on immigration that focused on the "immigration problem," but made no mention of the efforts by immigrant workers and advocates to organize and advocate for their human rights. Furthermore, NCCIR had recently organized a press conference to announce the release of a groundbreaking report on precisely what the newspaper's piece had left out: Hard evidence on the violent treatment of immigrants during immigrant raids *(see "Case study: Releasing a report," page 69)*. Despite an invitation, the paper was a no-show at the press conference where this report was announced.

Bacon and NCCIR saw these two media mishaps as an opportunity to place an opinion editorial. Bacon recounts: "This prompted me to call the op ed editor. We voiced our grievance with the series and the lack of coverage of the press conference." Bacon wrote the following op ed, which the paper ran.
—Seeta Peña Gangadharan

Immigration laws abused

Tuesday, October 20, 1998

There is an immigration crisis in the United States, but it is not caused by uncontrolled borders or too many immigrants. It is a sweatshop crisis—the unjust enforcement of immigration law that is bringing back conditions in the workplace reminiscent of a century ago.

David Bacon
Board Member
Northern California Coalition
for Immigrant Rights
995 Market Street, Ste. 1108
San Francisco, CA 94103
(P) 415 243-8215
(F) 415 243-8628
(E) nccir@igc.org
www.nccir.org

Undocumented workers pump $63 billion into the California economy. Whole industries make large profits on immigrant labor. But workers themselves only receive a small percentage of it. Meanwhile, immigration raids and employer sanctions undermine the ability of immigrant workers to fight for better pay and treatment. Even more disturbing, as immigrant workers have sought to organize unions, employers have used immigration law, often with the cooperation of the federal government, to stop them.

A report issued this week by the National Network for Immigrant and Refugee Rights on the impact of immigration raids details case after case in which immigration enforcement has been used to deny immigrants their workplace rights:
• In Silicon Valley, Shine Building Maintenance used a check of workers' immigration documents as a pretext to fire its pro-union workforce during an organizing drive.

- Last year in San Leandro, the Mediacopy factory, in cooperation with the Immigration and Naturalization Service (INS), used threats of document checks to terrorize workers before a union election. Ninety-nine people were picked up for deportation.
- Last year, a federal court upheld the firing of a pro-union garment worker in New York, Gloria Montero, after the company's lawyer called the INS on its own pro-union workers during an organizing drive. A federal judge ruled this was legal.

Employer sanctions require employers to demand immigration documents from workers. But document verification has become an increasingly common employer tactic to stop union organizing.

Federal law says all employees, regardless of status, have union rights. But an employer doesn't have to rehire a worker it fires for union activity, if that worker is undocumented. In the San Francisco Bay area, immigration raids keep wages low. Raids focus on low-wage jobs—fast food workers, car wash employees and day laborers.

The fear of raids keeps workers from demanding higher wages, undermining everyone in these occupations—immigrants and native-born workers alike. Federal law says all workers are entitled to mandatory minimum wage and overtime, regardless of immigration status. But employer sanctions keep workers from enforcing that law, too.

In 1992, the INS signed a memorandum of understanding with the Department of Labor, requiring inspectors to turn over the names of undocumented workers who call them about wage and hour violations. A Department of Labor survey shows that less than 40 percent of licensed garment factories in Southern California pay the federally mandated minimum wage and overtime. Yet in Los Angeles, the INS initiated a series of raids against sweatshop workers, called Operation Buttonhole, based on information from Department of Labor inspectors.

When workers can't assert their rights, their wages drop. According to UCLA professor Goetz Wolff, the average hourly wage of California women garment workers fell from $6.37 in 1988, when employer sanctions became part of federal law, to $5.62 five years later. Deteriorating wages in Los Angeles and Bay area sweatshops hurts the economy of our whole community. California labor believes that the use of immigration law as a weapon against workers must be stopped, especially the memorandum of understanding between the INS and the Department of Labor.

—David Bacon

Letters to the editor

Make them short and concise: one hundred fifty to 200 words, or less than one typed, double-spaced page. The sentences and paragraphs should be even shorter than in op eds.

Write no more than three or four short paragraphs. The first paragraph cites any previous coverage of a story: "In the January 2 issue of *The Daily Courier* you reported that..." The second paragraph introduces something personal and states your side of the argument: "As a person born and raised here in Our Town, I believe that..." The third paragraph moves the key messages—the same ones communicated in your press releases. The fourth and final paragraph gives a "kicker" to the letter.

Sign all letters and provide a phone number. Most media will not run unsigned letters and will call to verify their authenticity. If confidentiality is an issue, you may request that your name is withheld from publication. However, first check your local paper's policy on this.

Personalize the letter! The best letters are those containing attention-getting information.

Submit the letter via postal mail, fax or e-mail, depending on your local media's preference. It is not necessary to contact the editor numerous times to check on the status of your piece. This annoys editors. One friendly "heads-up" call is sufficient.

Remember that space is limited on the letters page; not every letter will run. Write your letter in a hard-hitting, personalized and concise manner. The chances of it running are much greater that way.

Consider writing "boiler plate" letters. In other words, compose standardized letters—that community folks in your "letters tree" can customize with their own personal information.

Encourage members of your community to write letters. Some people are letter factories and will submit one after another. Do not go overboard, but keep the letters coming.

Finally, remember that letters to the editor are one tool in your media kit. They are not the be-all and end-all of your media plan. Scoring a letter is valuable, but not as valuable as the front page feature and the op ed. Go for the grand slam: a feature, an op ed, an editorial *and* a slew of letters.

Letter to the editor example
Musical jobs

Jobs with Justice, a labor rights organization based in Washington, DC (see Case study: "Developing and moving key messages, page 27), composed the following boiler plate letters to the editor. These were included in their Day of Action media kit and distributed to every organization in the JWJ coalition. These examples were adapted accordingly by each group and then sent to local papers to be printed in the letters section.

The welfare reform debate in (Your State) has been filled with talk about dignity through work and replacing dependence with independence. The problem is that all of this rhetoric fails to address a question near and dear to the hearts of working people, like myself, across the state. Where will welfare recipients go when federal law mandates they move into jobs or they reach their lifetime limits?

There is a gap in (Your State) between the projected (Your State) job creation numbers over the next two years and the number of people federal welfare reform mandates must move from welfare to work in the coming year of more than (insert figure from National Report) jobs. The honest, reform-minded and hard working citizen must ask, "Where will all these people go and where will I end up?"

The nightmare of this version of welfare reform is that when working America wakes up to it we will discover that the federal welfare reform law is playing the music for an horrific game of musical jobs. This is what Lucy Smith in NJ discovered when she was laid off from her job of seven years at DSS only to be returned to that same position as a workfare placement for less money and without benefits. I'm sure plenty of people here in Ohio are worried about this same tragedy striking their family.

Unless the $3 billion in welfare to work money, and more, is spent frugally and precisely on a job creation campaign that meets family and community needs, then 1998 will come and go without any meaningful improvement in the welfare system. It is imperative that we give the job creation efforts from Wisconsin to California and from Philadelphia to Birmingham our support—and that we make sure the same programs are put into place here.

You're on the air
Doing radio and TV talk shows

Radio and TV talk shows can give you a powerful platform to communicate your messages. On the other hand, doing the talk show circuit—especially the "shock news" programs—can be unnerving to say the least. By all means, if you have tough skin, do the shows. Here are some tips for enhancing your performance.

Remember, most point-counterpoint talk shows are all heat and no light—and that's the nice shows! The shock-jock shows are all flame. In other words, expect confrontation that will most likely not be in the form of a polite debate. In fact, producers want the heat. Some shows, such as *Crossfire*, will allow debate and point-counterpoint statements. The *Geraldo*-like talk shows want the fights! So brace yourself.

Be prepared. What do you know about your opponent? Can you get any dirt? In fact, if the show *really* wants you, try to negotiate about who you will appear with—and who you will not. Can you leverage your position to ensure no "bottom feeders" will be on with you? For example, one AIDS activist refused to debate the hate monger Rev. Fred Phelps of Topeka, Kansas—the guy who pickets AIDS funerals with signs screaming, "Fag Dies of AIDS." But he did agree to go on a show with other right-wing arch-conservative representatives.

Be poised, comfortable and confident. The audience will better relate to you.

Be brief. You will not have the opportunity to educate everyone about all of the fine points of your issue, so do not even try. Get to the point fast and stay on message. If you can communicate three points during a 30-minute show, you will have done a good job.

Humor goes a long way. If you can inject humor in the form of a funny soundbite or disarmingly glib quote, go for it. You will probably win over audience members.

Be forceful. Do not wait for "your turn" to speak. Jump in and mix it up. Score a few zingers and your opponent will become destabilized.

Try not to be a policy wonk on the air. Personalize your statements with some warmth or friendly candor, it will win the studio and television audience to your side.

Most importantly, focus on key messages. Since you will have only a few times to actually speak—and then only a few seconds—have your messages in mind before going on the air and stick to them. Discipline the message. Do not let your opponent "shock" you with some outrageous statement designed to pull you off message. Do not try to answer every point and counterpoint.

Smile, you're on camera: Being "telegenic"

Television is the most powerful medium, reaching the most people. It is imperative to score TV coverage for your news. Your events should be designed with photo ops in mind. Your performance on television will carry tremendous weight. It will give you an extremely powerful platform from which to communicate your messages.

Here are some tips for being on TV:

• Fashion tips: For serious news–such as releasing a new report–avoid garish costumes, bright patterns, clashing colors and big jewelry. Notice how female correspondents never wear drop earrings–nor do the male reporters for that matter. If you feel comfortable in a suit or suitable "business" attire, it pays to wear it. For news made at rallies, vigils and other spontaneous events, clothing can be more attention-getting. *A rule*: Always wear what is appropriate, will present you professionally and will not distract from the news. Skip the buttons and pins since nobody will be able to read them. Viewers will just wonder what dropped on your lapel. Of course, if "street theater" is involved to dramatize your news, costumes are appropriate.

• Use makeup if necessary. If you get lucky and book yourself on consecutive studio talk shows, apply foundation or powder–to keep you from "shining"–before making the rounds.

• Use natural hand gestures that do not distract. Well-placed hand gestures will visually punctuate a point. But be careful, do not go overboard. All anyone will notice are your hands flapping around wildly. Avoid the "fig leaf" position–hands overlapping each other in front of your crotch. Do not put your hands in your pocket. It makes you slouch and is bad body language. Do not stand "at attention" with your hands firmly locked behind you. This is too stiff and too formal. Keep your hands relaxed at your sides, or better yet, gesture softly with them. People of faith are terrific at hand gestures. Watch the televangelists to pick up some pointers. Clergy members naturally bring their hands together, open their palms warmly, touch their hearts and thrust their fists. Take note. It looks great on TV!

• Nervous "twitches" are magnified. Every blink, "uh," "um," "duh," "ya know," and "like…" will be highly distracting.

• Relax. Ground yourself. Breathe. Try to remain composed and poised.

• If you make a mistake, stop and start over–unless, of course, it is live TV. If it is being taped, just do another take if you stumble. But do not take all day. By the 15th take, the reporter will probably get impatient.

• Add a personal inflection to your quotes. Let something personal–a spark, a warm intimacy, a sensitivity–come through your eyes. That is where the audience will be looking. One seasoned activist and veteran of TV soundbites can make his eyes moist on command. Hey, if it works on TV, why not!

• Do not look at the camera; look at the reporter. Reporters want an informal, conversational tone. The exception to this rule is if you are being "patched in" from one studio to another. If that is the case you *will* stare at a camera, its red light glowing, with a microphone hidden in your ear and a disembodied voice whispering cues to you from some invisible command center. Try to look natural and sparkle for the camera.

• Do not be distracted by the reporter or the crew. Even if all hell breaks loose behind you–or the reporter keeps looking at her watch or writing in a notebook–stay focused on communicating your messages.

• Do not repeat the question in your answer or use the words of your oppressor in your soundbite. "Welfare cheats? Welfare cheats? This isn't about welfare cheats!" Wrong. If you mentioned "welfare cheats" three times in your statement, it *is* about welfare cheats. Make sure to stick to your key messages. Also, do not take up valuable soundbite seconds to state your name and organization in your quote. Your name and affiliation will be included, either superimposed beneath you on the screen or announced by the correspondent.

• Most importantly, respond with your key messages. Make sure you get the message out no matter what the question is. Do not let the question throw you off. Discipline the message.

• Remember, the viewing audience is the target–not the journalist, the camera crew or the studio staff. Therefore, do not address the reporter personally. Leave the "happy talk" to the anchor people. Even though you are looking at the reporter and not the camera, use your voice and presence to reach right into the living rooms, bars and airport waiting lounges of your audience and proudly proclaim that we are not going to take it anymore!–or at least move your key messages.

Spokesperson training

Set up a community spokesperson practice session. All you need is a video camera, VCR and television set. In the 50's and 60's Tupperware parties were the rage; now in the 90's it is soundbite soirées. Brief folks on the message, rehearse their soundbites, then tape them. Play the tape back and critique it. Though slightly nerve-wracking, you will find it fun and educational–and it will boost your spokespersons' self confidence. Besides, this is only practice (*see "Being a better spokesperson" and "You're on the air," pages 33 and 75*).

76

News radio
Getting the word out using radio actualities

If you could stir them from their sleep and speak to thousands of your fellow citizens as they get ready for work in the morning, or have their undivided attention as they drive to their jobs, you would probably think it was a great opportunity to inform them about an important issue of the day that could affect their lives. With radio news, often heard through alarm clocks, in car radios and on people's desks at work, one can do just that.

Many Americans get their news from the radio. In fact, Americans listen to the radio about three hours per day, on average, according to the Radio Advertising Bureau. Whether it's heard through an alarm clock, over coffee and toast or through car radios, most Americans get their morning news from the radio. Half of Americans listen to the radio at work, while three out of four adults listen in their cars.

While some stations have "all news" or "all talk" formats, many more incorporate news into their regular broadcasts, with newscasts at the top and bottom of the hour (on the hour and half hour). These newscasts are often a combination of national news from a news service such as ABC or UPI, and local news produced by the station. The local newscasts can be an important media target for an advocacy organization with news to convey.

Radio news reaches many Americans in unique and powerful ways. This important segment of the media should be incorporated into a comprehensive media outreach campaign.

There are essentially three ways in which an advocacy group can get its news on the radio. First, it can try to get radio stations to send someone from its news department to cover the media event (news conference, rally, etc.). Unfortunately, this approach is limited, as only the biggest news radio stations have more than one person on their news staffs. Second, an organization can try to get members of the news staffs at local radio stations to conduct short interviews by phone with the group's spokesperson about the event. This is also a better strategy with stations with slightly larger news staffs, since they can afford the time it takes to conduct a short "newser." It is also limited by how much time a spokesperson can spend on the phone on the day of an event, when the news is timely.

For a news story with a statewide or larger focus, there is a third approach: Radio actualities, also known as radio newsfeeds, allow an organization to reach many radio stations in one morning with a pre-recorded news story. This cost effective approach also has limitations. Usually, the biggest news stations will not use actualities, as they consider them spoon-fed news. Some of the smallest stations do not have the equipment necessary to record actualities over the phone. This leaves a large number of mid-sized stations to target for actuality distribution.

Radio actualities are essentially mini-press releases for the radio. Just like a news story that airs on the radio, they include an announcer summarizing the story and introducing the spokesperson, who delivers a colorful "soundbite" about the story, including any appropriate data being released.

Actualities are created at a recording studio and professionally transferred onto audio cassette tapes that—with the use of inexpensive equipment—can be recorded by radio stations from your telephone. To deliver an actuality, someone must call the news department of a particular radio station, successfully pitch the story, and play the tape until it completes its run, usually about 60 seconds. After rewinding the tape, the process is repeated.

Radio actualities are a fairly inexpensive and very effective way to get a message out to a broad cross section of people in a state. The organization writes, records and disseminates the actuality, thereby retaining control of the message.

Excerpted from Making Radio Work for You, *published by the Families USA Foundation. (See "Books publications and Web sites in "Resources," page 117.)*

Families USA Foundation
1334 G Street, NW
Washington, DC 20005
(P) 202 628-3030
(F) 202 347-2417
(E) info@familiesusa.org
www.familiesusa.org

77

Using the Internet

Seeta Peña Gangadharan

Whether you are a technophobe or technophile, developing a Web presence is important to consider when doing media work.

In this short piece we provide useful information to help you determine why and how to make effective use of the Internet as part of your media campaigns. Included here are facts and figures on online media outlets, in particular newspapers; how reporters use the Internet; how a few nonprofits have successfully mobilized media coverage with the help of the Internet; and which progressive Web developers or consultant groups can advise and work with you, should you decide to pursue a greater Internet profile. We include the Web addresses of numerous news services.

News online: what is out there for activists

As the Web becomes a more popular communication medium the media is realizing its importance and moving to a digital format. According to a study by the *American Journalism Review*, as of 1998 more than 2,050 U.S. newspapers were published online. That is 1,305 more than in the previous year. Moreover, journalists use the Web as a means of exhibiting their work and connecting with their readers. By printing e-mail addresses in bylines, journalists encourage people to use the Internet.

Online newspapers, however, are only one way the news gets posted on the Web. News links are featured on portal sites or gateways and enable you to access a myriad of topics, services or products. Many Web search engines, such as Yahoo! and Excite have become portal sites, because they provide you with e-mail service, chat rooms or discussion groups in addition to news links. Other examples of portals are paid services, such as America Online (AOL). News links are found on a front page (the welcome page that pops up straight away when you log onto a site). For example, AOL (www.aol.com), Internet Explorer (www.microsoft.com/ie), Institute for Global Communications (www.igc.org), and even other smaller Internet service providers (ISPs), prominently feature up-to-date news headlines.

Every search engine—such as Yahoo! (www.yahoo.com), Excite (www.excite.com), HotBot (www.hotbot.com) and Infoseek (www.infoseek.com)—have a special link, often titled "Today's News" or "Today's Headlines."

While online news alerts and links are increasingly visible, the originating source of the news is often not so "new." News outlets—such as the Associated Press (www.ap.com), Washington Post (www.washingtonpost.com), British Broadcasting Services (www.bbs.com), Reuters (www.reuters.com) and USA Today (www.usatoday.com)—all provide content to Web search engines on a direct-feed basis. Therefore, search engines often have a story before the items even hit the newsstand. There have been a number of recent cases where stories have been broken online.

If you want to see your story "featured" on the front page of portal sites, such as Excite, AOL or even IGC, you need to find out which news outlets provide them with content. Contact the online directors/editors of these outlets directly.

For Example: Bacon's Media Directory *(see "Media sources" in the Resources section, page 111)* catalogs the contact information of online editors at major media outlets. You can also directly contact the main editorial department of a media outlet to find out the contact information.

You can also approach editors at online media outlets. A few examples include: the Drudge Report (www.drudge.com), State (www.state.com), Salon (www.salon.com) and Common Dreams (www.commondreams.com).

Do not contact the Web search engines or Internet Service Providers, since none of them—except for Yahoo!—will understand what you are talking about. (Occasionally, Yahoo! takes suggestions from individuals who post to their web address or url (www.yahoo.com/news) and notify Yahoo! editors of interesting and relevant news links that should be listed under "Today's Headlines.")

Using a Web site

Your site can include vast amounts of information—as long as it is easily accessible. Once reporters know your Web address, they can use the information repeatedly to augment their coverage of your issue.

Children Now (www.childrennow.org), a nonpartisan group that advocates for positive change for children and families, employs a strategic approach to the Internet. They provide a vast array of information on their site with broad appeal for anyone, including members of the press or the curious Web surfer. Always current with its latest updates on children's issues, Children Now makes available every report or publication they have produced. Furthermore, visitors may subscribe directly to monthly action alerts to receive updates on legislation or resources relevant to children's issues.

The overall effect is powerful. Winning several awards for the quality of its content and its resource listings—or links—Children Now is on the new media "radar."

Michael Stein, Internet coordinator at Children Now, offers instructive comments on maintaining a Web presence:

"Most groups wonder, 'Why should we develop a Web site when only three or four people are going to look at it?' Well, the type of work you do online is more than likely to be received in the same manner as your regular, tried-and-true media strategizing techniques. For example, for every 300 press releases you send out, you will have to follow up with at least 150 phone calls. The Web site can get information out fast and in a timely way, with little follow-up required."

In other words, though the net result from your Internet efforts may seem nominal at first—only a handful of "page visits" or "hits"—any reporter now has easy access to your group's information.

Through your Web site you can provide:
- Previous press releases and press clips.
- Background information on your organization.
- Data, charts and graphics such as photos and illustrations.
- A search engine to comb your site's archives.
- Subscriptions to a listserve that sends out weekly e-mail alerts to reporters and interested readers.
- Subscriptions to a listserve action alerts, which ask constituents for a specific action to be taken on a current political issue or campaign.
- and much more.

Resources and links

Several Web sites cater directly to the social change community by consolidating the online progressive world. Other Web sites maintain their link pages to progressive sites on a regular basis.

Creating your Web site

✔ Make your site informational. Include as much useful background information about an issue as prudent, and keep the site updated. Do not forget your mission statement and, most importantly, contact information.

✔ Make sure your Web site is well-designed. Information must be easily accessible.

✔ Archive material on your Web site. This makes it a more useful resource for reporters.

✔ Mention your Web site wherever your organization's name appears, such as stationery letterhead.

✔ Update your Web site to reflect changes in your organization's media efforts. Highlight the latest press release prominently.

✔ Build broadcast lists—alerts, listserves or online newsletters—that highlight information on your Web site.

✔ Develop connections with other Web sites; exchange links.

✔ Register your Web site with all search engines and progressive Internet directories: Institute for Global Communications (www.igc.org), Web Directory (www.Webdirectory.com), WebActive (http://www.webactive.com), Hands Net (www.handsnet.org), Consumer Net (www.consumernet.org), Mining Co. (http://www.about.com) and People Link (www.peoplelink.com).

✔ Talk to your Internet provider to obtain usage statistics for your Web site. Do a quarterly review of what content is popular. Make changes accordingly and let your readers know what is new.

Here are a few areas to visit for resources that may be useful for you. Consider entering your group on their growing list of links.

∎ The Institute for Global Communications (IGC) (www.igc.org): provides a complete listing of alternative media outlets online.

∎ Idealist (www.idealist.org): a clearing house of nonprofit and volunteering resources

∎ Common Dreams (www.commondreams.org): a site that features breaking news and views for progressive-thinking Americans.

∎ WebActive (www.webactive.com): a weekly publication designed to offer progressive activists an up-to-date resource to find other organizations and individuals on the Web with similar values and interests.

∎ Protest.Net (www.protest.net): a site to help progressive activists by providing a central place where the times and locations of protests and meetings can be posted.

As with the mainstream media, many progressive news sites usually duplicate their print versions for the Web. Access to news stories is sometimes limited or subscription fees required for full view of the online version. For example, Utne Reader's Web site (www.utne.com) has enjoyed success using this formula while simultaneously providing chat rooms and other services to progressive minds online.

Conclusion

If you think that developing a Web presence is the least of your organization's priorities, think again. The online profile of your organization should always be included in your media plan. Having an effective Web site means the ability to provide reporters and the general public with important and timely information. Remember to check out the Resources Section at the end of this book to find out who can help you develop, design or maintain your Web site.

Case study
A resource for reporters

The Internet is a time-saving research resource, especially for reporters looking for background or hoping to communicate quickly with sources.

Josh Karliner works with the Transnational Resource Action Center, or TRAC/Corporate Watch (www.corpwatch.org), a nonprofit organization that fights for corporate accountability. Of all their corporate watchdog projects, TRAC's efforts to expose unfair factory labor practices by the Nike Corporation garnered the widest media attention.

TRAC's campaign against Nike underscored the usefulness of maintaining an online presence. TRAC made all documents essential for covering the Nike story available on the Web. TRAC's Web site featured reports on labor conditions in Nike factories as well as all background information about TRAC/Corporate Watch and its previous work. TRAC also concentrated on the various links it could exchange with other Web sites.

Josh Karliner
Executive Director
Transnational Resource Action
Center/Corporate Watch
P.O. Box 29344
San Francisco, CA 94129
(P) 415 561.6567
(F) 415 561.6493
(E) corpwatch@org
www.corpwatch.org

Through online communication, TRAC emphasized its relationship with the press. Realizing the efficiency of e-mail and reporters' appetite for quick information, TRAC concentrated on developing a database of reporters' e-mail addresses. Because not all reporters work with e-mail, lists take time to develop. But the effect was rewarding. TRAC currently boasts of an e-mail press list of more than 100 reporters and a listserve of 2,000 recipients for their weekly alerts.

TRAC met with great success in their campaign against Nike. Following their use of the Internet (and traditonal media campaigning), TRAC forced Nike to announce that they would investigate and improve labor conditions of workers in overseas factories.

As a result, reporters have come to accept TRAC as a legitimate news source. Now, when reporters from *Business Week*, the *Wall Street Journal* or the *New York Times* who previously worked on the Nike story need to research corporate accountability issues, TRAC is a group they know to approach. Similarly, TRAC continues to be in contact with reporters they culled from their intensive media work, keeping their database informed of what's going on with their issues.

Working with PR consultants

At some point in your media planning you may realize there is simply too much important news to make with too few people in-house to make it. Depending on your budget or ability to raise media funds, that may be the time to consider retaining professional public relations consultation.

Engaging PR consultants reflects a higher level of media sophistication in an organization. This section provides guidance in working with consultants to make sure you get what you want and the consultant understands your needs.

More and more organizations are turning to professional public relations consultants for assistance with publicizing their issues. These media professionals can help you garner increased media attention and do follow-up work.

You can hire an individual consultant working as a PR specialist or a large PR firm—which can potentially offer you a broader array of services. Working with PR consultants can be a beneficial experience or a frustrating one depending on your media plan, the information you have about the consultant and what the consultant knows about you.

Before hiring a consultant

Consider the following four-step process before you consider retaining a consultant:

- Do an internal capacity assessment. Can your organization sustain increased media work and attention: working with the consultant, responding to media inquiries and possibly being in a prolonged media "campaign mode" with deadlines and demands?
- Ask yourself: Do we need PR help? Can media work be handled in-house? Is media-savvy staff available to do the job and still perform their other duties?
- Determine your news. Despite the best intentions of some consultants to "manufacture" news, only work with a PR consultant if your organization has something new to communicate.
- Identify your goals and create a plan. It is critical that you have clear goals and a strategic media plan in mind for your media work.

When creating your media plan you should consider the following:

- The estimated duration of the campaign.
- What you want accomplished in terms of media hits. Do you want major national media placement with local coverage?
- What you want accomplished for general exposure. Do you want to increase awareness about an issue with emphasis on moving key policy leaders?
- Your target audience: is it youth, people of color, lawmakers, etc?
- The scope of your campaign: is it national, national plus local or regional, multi-city action or local only?

Media goals and parameters

If you hire a consultant, she or he most likely will provide feedback and suggest bigger goals or a more realistic plan. A typical media campaign involving a professional PR consultant might have the following goals:

- The campaign will be for one month. The campaign's finale will be the introduction of Bill XYZ in the state legislature—or the rollout of the report, or a mass visibility action, etc.—with attendant press conferences and briefings.
- Maximum media exposure in national and/or regional-local mainstream media, with significant media coverage in "issue" and "niche" media—environmental press, women's media, government talk show—and the alternative press. This includes at least three or more "hits" in major dailies in select urban markets and a possible "hit" on a national radio and/or TV talk show, plus a hit on a wire service.

■ The capacity to inform leading policy-makers in your field about your report and your issue. Your messages, therefore, must be crafted to resonate with this audience.

Caveats to consider

Doing media work necessitates having a big picture view and understanding that it will be a process. Major policy change and significant media transformation does not happen overnight. There is no "magic media bullet" in media work. It is never possible to predict precisely what reporter or media outlet will go for a story—no matter how good the PR consultant.

Finally, you must realize that media work—whether in-house or contracted out—takes resources. It is critically important to incorporate media strategy into your program plan and fundraising proposals. *Plan* for your media. It will not happen on its own.

So, who do we hire?

It can be important to work with a consultant—whether an individual or a firm—that shares your political and cultural beliefs on some level. It is also key to retain a consultant with the necessary media connections and resources. Before signing a contract, ask your consultant the following series of questions:

■ What are their media contacts, including print, magazine, radio, TV, alternative media and "niche" media? In what media markets are they strong?

■ Can you see copies of news clips from past clients?

■ Can you check their references?

■ Can you see an example of a successful media strategy and messages of previous clients? Can they help you shape *your* messages?

■ Can you examine press kits and other materials?

■ Are they cyber savvy? How will they use the Internet, Web pages and e-mail to publicize your message?

■ Who are their clients? Do they represent people from the opposition, thus setting up a possible conflict of interest?

■ Do they personally support the politics of your project on some level?

■ Finally, is the PR consultant *creative?* Can they come up with clever ideas for getting you press?

List of PR consultants

The SPIN Project makes available a list of PR firms with which we are familiar. This list is not exclusive by any means and it changes frequently. SPIN does not endorse any company on this list, but our experience suggests they may be in tune with your political goals. (*See "Resources," page 110 for a list of PR/media consultants*)

Shop around for a PR consultant. Ask a few consultants to submit proposals. Give them guidelines for what kind of media campaign you want. Ask for references. Then call to get their feedback.

What does it cost?

There is no set formula for what a consultant will charge and what you get for the money. At a minimum expect to spend at least $5,000 for a basic media effort. This might include placing and pitching stories, producing the press kit and arranging interviews—among other tasks. More prestigious and/or experienced consultants will charge more, ostensibly to take advantage of their greater media access.

One environmental justice group signed a contract for nearly $20,000 for a major multiple-week campaign that included story placement in key national media. Another organization spent about $7,000 for a shorter campaign that scored them a handful of good media hits locally and nationally.

The price will depend on the duration of the contract, the specific tasks you agree on, the prominence of the firm and your media goals.

One suggested component of any media contract is an **exit clause**. This allows you to drop the PR firm if they are not delivering what you want by a certain deadline—and might decide a consultant is not right at all.

What will the consultant do for us?

From the outset it is critical you be clear and explicit with the consultant as to exactly what you want done and what the consultant *can* do for you. The following are a few tasks you can expect PR consultants to perform. As part of your contract they may be responsible for all or some of these tasks. At a minimum, you should negotiate these with the firm and know what will be included in the cost.

You can expect a PR consultant to:

■ Assist in creating and/or implementing your **strategic media plan**.

■ Help you **frame the issue** for maximum media interest and help you craft **strategic media messages.**

■ Write and distribute **press releases and media advisories**. Be clear on the editing process—approvals, feedback, turn-around schedule—and deadlines for drafts. Will they develop the media list?

■ Produce "media deliverables"—specifically the **press kit** and **backgrounders**.

■ Draft or edit your **opinion editorial** and place it.

■ Make **pitch calls** to reporters.

■ Book radio/TV **talk shows.**

■ Organize **media briefings**.

■ Stage and publicize **media events** and handle the press in attendance.

■ Other tasks may include: helping launch a **Web site**; training key **spokespersons**; handling and prioritizing reporters' **calls**; producing **video press releases** or radio reports; following up with **reporters**; maintaining **clip service;** and giving you copies of media hits, including broadcast transcripts.

Staff contact with consultant

In day-to-day dealings, have one key staff person be the interface with the consultant. PR consultants get frustrated when they must go to several people in an organization for approvals, input and so forth. Schedule regular check-in meetings with the PR agent handling your account to review progress. Create a timeline for deadlines and deliverables—and stick to it. During the "hottest" part of the campaign, expect to be in touch with the consultant several times a day. The consultant may move into your office or close by on the big day to handle media inquiries and other activities. Following the campaign, debrief with the consultant and track media coverage to assess if your goals were attained.

Working with professional PR consultants can be a rewarding experience that results in a successful media campaign and media coverage for your issue. The best consultants want their clients to succeed and feel proud of their work on your behalf. Treat your consultant professionally and with respect, and they will help you do a terrific job in the press.

Reprinted from the SPIN Project brochure, "Working With PR Consultants, A Primer for Nonprofit Social Change Groups."

PR consultants at work

In August 1998, the Center for Health, Environment and Justice (CHEJ) was handed a media opportunity that would make most national and grassroots activists envious: A major "20 years later" type of news hook with dramatic national and local press campaign potential. At the same time, the moment caused anxiety and posed several questions among the CHEJ staff about how to handle the media. CHEJ's situation offers a case study in working with public-relations consultants and maximizing your media bang.

The scene

CHEJ works on issues of environmental justice and the effects of toxic pollution on American communities and neighborhoods. August 1998 marked the 20th anniversary of the Love Canal Crisis in Niagara Falls, New York. The crisis—one of the biggest toxic pollution debacles in American history—erupted around a hazardous waste site that was leaking into a working-class, blue-collar community. Folks in Love Canal joined together in a David vs. Goliath fight for the total relocation of all 90 families who lived near the dump. I was a member of one of those families and now serve as executive director and a founder of CHEJ.

The dilemma and the scope

The anniversary served as the national hook for a massive media, public education and organizing campaign to frame the issue into contemporary times and move updated messages. CHEJ planned media events in different cities across the country from April until October. Meanwhile, I released a book about Love Canal to coincide with the anniversary. A National Day of Action involving 75 groups in at least 18 states was also unleashed.

The main problem was that staff resources at CHEJ were limited. Like staff at similar groups, CHEJ employees were stretched to the max. Would CHEJ be able to pull off such an ambitious campaign or would this be a major missed media opportunity?

The internal debate

Staff and executive leadership at CHEJ debated long and hard about how to handle the situation. Two choices emerged: Either hire a PR firm to handle press or hire someone to come on staff as a full-time CHEJ media person. The group did not have an in-house PR position. Money was budgeted for the media. The question was who would do it?

Some staff argued they could do the media

work internally. Others strongly believed they could not do it alone and needed outside help. To complicate the matter, the organization had an unpleasant experience with a previous PR consultant, who, among other things, sent scientifically inaccurate press releases to reporters and did not seem to connect to the issues. Staff still regretted that experience.

The pros and cons of going outside were examined. Since hiring a PR specialist would mean the organization would not have to ride out a huge learning curve for a new PR staffer, and—most importantly—the already overworked staff would not have this huge project dumped on them, CHEJ ultimately decided to bring in a professional PR consultant.

To accomplish an ambitious media agenda, CHEJ hired a professional PR firm, Pro-Media, based in New York. CHEJ wanted a firm that: understood organizing campaign media work, had a good track record with and access to national journalists, would be willing to work on a month-to-month basis for the duration of the effort, would work with local leaders partnering with us on our message and had creative thinkers who could view the issue "outside the box."

The consultant

CHEJ approached the process of hiring a PR consultant both strategically and deliberately. We had already learned from our previous experience and were determined not to make the same mistakes.

Tough questions were asked of the consultant and commitments gotten on the table right at the beginning. The SPIN Project worked with CHEJ to prepare us to engage the consultant and helped us understand what was possible—right down to the contract stipulations.

The key stipulations were:

• A clear *commitment* to the project and CHEJ. Realizing the PR firm would have other clients, CHEJ demanded the firm provide ongoing high-level support. This came in response to the previous PR consultant who, at times, seemed to care more about other clients than CHEJ.
• A clear sense of *accountability and reporting structure*. CHEJ wanted not only the firm's commitment for the long haul, but an agreement that the organization would work with only one or two persons at the firm. This would allow for a working

Lois Gibbs
Executive Director
Center for Health, Environment and Justice
P.O. Box 6806
Falls Church, VA 22040
(P) 703 237-2249
(F) 703 237-7449
(E) cchw@essential.org
www.essential.org/cchw

continuity and keep CHEJ from having to stop and reeducate new consultants as they came on to the account.
• A good *grassroots sensitivity*. Knowing that the consultant would be working with folks in the field, CHEJ needed to have a high level of trust in the firm.
• Clearly articulated *responsibilities*. Among other tasks, the PR consultant would help produce press kits, develop spokespersons, set up media briefings and breakfasts and pitch and place stories. Placing the story—particularly in the national media—was understood to be one of the consultant's key jobs. Meanwhile, CHEJ would focus on organizing and outreach to community activists and set up local media events working with the local groups. CHEJ would also pick up and handle the reporters who got the story off the wires as it unfolded.
• The *final OK* on all media documentation would be left to CHEJ. Nothing would be sent out without clearance.
• Clear understanding of the *duration of the campaign*. In this case, the main part of the campaign lasted for three months.
• For all this, CHEJ would pay between *$5,000 and $7,000 a month*. In January, a full seven months before the anniversary, CHEJ worked with the PR consultant to draft a contract. The dotted line was signed and CHEJ was in business.

The message
One of the consultant's responsibilities was to help CHEJ refine the message: "Twenty years after the Love Canal crisis we are finding the same chemicals that families tried to escape from, on the tables, in the food and in the homes of the American people. Instances of childhood cancer, birth defects and learning disorders are on the rise in children while infertility and cancer are increasing in adults. While the American people are facing a serious public health crisis, the polluter industry continues to make huge profits. Twenty years after Love Canal we now know enough to act."

The outcome
The results of their media work were terrific. CHEJ spokespersons did more than 140 interviews with national, regional and local media. At the national level, the *Washington Post*, *USA Today*, *Good*

Morning America, *CBS Sunday*, *CBS Morning News*, *CNN Headline News*, *Fox Headline* and NPR—to name just a few—all went for the story and editorials. A host of national magazines—from *Family Circle* and *Redbook*, to *George* and *Working Mother*—did pieces on the anniversary as well. The list of local media that did local stories was too long to itemize. A breakfast briefing for women's media—set up by the PR consultant—was a big success in reaching one of our target audiences. The children's health angle of the story—"Kids and chemicals in your own backyard: Love Canal lives on"—also provided a great hook for reporters.

Countless people called to inform us the Love Canal story was everywhere. In some areas, you could not turn on the TV or radio, or read a newspaper without hearing about the issue.

If we had to do it again
The experience for both the client and the consultant was very positive. However, there was, of course, room for improvement.
• The PR consultant emphasized the need to find local stories to keep the issue fresh for reporters. Identifying compelling grassroots folks and finding new "spokesmodels" every time a reporter from a new location called was labor-intensive work and kept CHEJ staff extremely busy. Often there was not enough time for CHEJ to brief all the "messengers." If we had to do it over again we would plan more for grassroots outreach, and put more emphasis on communicating the messages earlier to the grassroots and developing more local spokespersons.
• The consultant was often frustrated when she had to call two or three folks at CHEJ to get information. Both sides agreed it was imperative to designate one key staff person as the main contact—much as we had stipulated in the consultant's contract. This would have made the communication process more effective and efficient.
• One gentle nudging the consultant often gave CHEJ was a reminder for national spokespeople to always mention the organization. According to the consultant, CHEJ sometimes did not promote itself enough.

—Lois Gibbs

4. Reacting to media

How to detect and fight bias in news media

Kim Deterline

This model for detecting and challenging media bias was originally produced for Fairness and Accuracy in Reporting (FAIR), a leading national media watchdog group that offers well-documented criticism of media bias and censorship. FAIR seeks to invigorate the First Amendment by advocating for greater diversity in the press. FAIR scrutinizes media practices that marginalize public interest, minority and dissenting viewpoints. The author, Kim Deterline, currently runs a nonprofit, progressive PR consulting group, We Interrupt This Message.

Media has tremendous power in setting cultural guidelines and in shaping political discourse. It is essential that news media, along with other institutions, are challenged to be fair and accurate. The first step in challenging biased news coverage is documenting bias. Here are some questions to ask yourself about newspaper, TV and radio news.

—Seeta Peña Gangadharan

Who are the sources?

Be aware of the political perspective of the sources used in a story. Media too often rely on "official"—government, corporate and establishment think tank—sources. For instance, FAIR found that in 40 months of *Nightline* programming the most frequent guests were Henry Kissinger, Alexander Haig, Elliott Abrams and Jerry Falwell. Progressive and public-interest voices were grossly underrepresented.

Kim Deterline
Director
We Interrupt This Message
965 Mission St., Ste. 220
San Francisco, CA 94110
(P) 415 905-4527
(F) 415 537-9439
(E) interrupt@igc.org

To portray issues fairly and accurately, media must broaden their spectrum of sources. Otherwise, they serve merely as megaphones for those already in power.

Count the number of corporate and government sources versus the number of progressive, public-interest, female and minority voices. Demand mass media expand their rolodexes. Better yet, give them lists of progressive and public-interest experts in the community.

Is there a lack of diversity?

What is the race and gender diversity at the news outlet you watch compared to the communities it serves? How many producers, editors or decision-makers at news outlets are women, people of color or openly gay or lesbian? In order to fairly represent different communities, news outlets should have members of those communities in decision-making positions.

How many of the experts cited by these news outlets are women and people of color? FAIR's 40-month survey of *Nightline* found that of the show's U.S. guests, 92 percent are white and 89 percent are male. A similar survey of PBS's *NewsHour* found its guest list to be 90 percent white, 87 percent male.

Demand the media reflect the diversity of the public they serve. Call or write media outlets every time you see an all-male or all-white panel of experts discussing issues that affect women and people of color.

From whose point of view is the news reported?

Political coverage often focuses on how issues affect politicians or corporate executives rather than those *directly* affected by the issue. For example, many stories on parental notification of abortion emphasized the "tough choice" confronting male politicians yet quoted no women under 18—those clearly with the most at stake in the debate. Similarly, economics coverage usually looks at how events impact stockholders rather than workers or consumers.

Demand that those affected by the issue have a voice in coverage. Identify and train people directly affected by the issue to be spokespersons, and provide their names and contact numbers to the media.

Are there double standards?

Do media hold some people to one standard while using a different standard for other groups? Youth of color who commit crimes are referred to as "predators," whereas adult criminals who commit white-collar crimes are often portrayed as having been tragically led astray. Think tanks partly funded by unions are often identified as "labor-backed" while think tanks heavily funded by business interests are usually not identified as "corporate-backed."

Expose the double standard by coming up with a parallel example or citing similar stories that were covered differently.

Do stereotypes skew coverage?

Does coverage of the drug crisis focus almost exclusively on African Americans, despite the fact that the vast majority of drug users are white? Does coverage of women on welfare focus overwhelmingly on African-American women, despite the fact that the majority of welfare recipients are not black? Are lesbians portrayed as "man-hating" and gay men portrayed as "sexual predators" (even though a child is 100 times more likely to be molested by a family member than by an unrelated gay adult— *Denver Post*, 9/28/92)?

Educate journalists about misconceptions involved in stereotypes, and about how stereotypes characterize individuals unfairly.

What are the unchallenged assumptions?

Often the most important message of a story is not explicitly stated. For instance, in coverage of women on welfare, the age at which a woman had her first child will often be reported—the implication being that the woman's sexual "promiscuity," rather than institutional economic factors, are responsible for her plight.

Coverage of rape trials will often focus on a woman's sexual history as though it calls her credibility into question. After the arrest of William Kennedy Smith, a *New York Times* article (4/17/91) dredged up a host of irrelevant personal details about his accuser, including the facts that she had skipped classes in the 9th grade, had received several speeding tickets and when on a date had talked to other men.

Challenge the assumption directly. Often bringing assumptions to the surface will demonstrate their absurdity. Most reporters, for example, will not say directly that a woman deserved to be raped because of what she was wearing.

Checklist for monitoring the media

If you decide to monitor a media outlet to chart coverage and expose bias, consider this check list.

- Choose a reasonable period of time to monitor a media outlet (2-3 months or more).

- Survey one or more media outlets for comparison purposes (if your community has more than one daily newspaper, for example).

- Count the number of times coverage appears and keep copies of all articles in a notebook.

- Document biases or inaccuracies (use tips in previous article for guidance).

- Keep track of news that is omitted. What events did you stage that were ignored, for example, yet the media found time to cover your opposition?

- Confirm data accuracy of your monitoring, then analyze and publish your conclusions in a report or notebook.

- Request a briefing with editors to present your findings and demand fair and balanced coverage.

89

Is the language loaded?

When media adopt loaded terminology they help shape public opinion. For instance, media often use the right-wing buzzword "racial preference" to refer to affirmative action programs. Polls show that this decision makes a huge difference in how the issue is perceived. A 1992 Louis Harris poll, for example, found that 70 percent said they favored "affirmative action" while only 46 percent favored "racial preference programs." For gay and lesbian people, phrases such as "special rights," "avowed homosexual" (are there "avowed heterosexuals?"), "innocent AIDS victim" (versus "guilty" victims?) and others reinforce misconceptions.

Demonstrate how the language chosen gives people an inaccurate impression of the issue, program or community.

Is there a lack of context?

Coverage of so-called "reverse discrimination" usually fails to focus on any of the institutional factors that give power to prejudice, such as larger issues of economic inequality and institutional racism. Coverage of hate speech against gays and lesbians often fails to mention increases in gay-bashing and how the two might be related.

Provide the context. Communicate to the journalist, or write a letter to the editor that includes the relevant information.

Do the headlines and stories match?

Usually headlines are not written by the reporter, but by an editor or copy editor. Since many people just skim headlines, misleading headlines have a significant impact. A classic case: In a *New York Times* article on the June 1988 U.S.-Soviet summit in Moscow, Margaret Thatcher was quoted as saying of Reagan, "Poor dear, there's nothing between his ears." The Times headline: "Thatcher Salute to the Reagan Years."

Call or write the newspaper and point out the contradiction.

Are stories on important issues featured prominently?

Look at where stories appear. Newspaper articles on the most widely read pages—the front pages and the editorial pages—and lead stories on television and radio will have the greatest influence on public opinion.

When you see a story on government officials engaged in activities that violate the Constitution buried on page A29, call the newspaper and object. Let the paper know how important you feel an issue is and demand that important stories get prominent coverage. Also, are corrections and retractions given equal play to the original mistake?

Fighting the media bias can be done as long as you remain vigilant and committed.

Excerpted from "Media Activism Kit" created by FAIR, the media watch group. Kim Deterline is a founder of the progressive PR consultant group, We Interrupt This Message.

A quick call that changed biased coverage

This is a brief tale highlighting how a little research, one letter and a phone call can alter coverage on a controversial issue. The author, Robin Kane, was then working at the National Gay and Lesbian Task Force (NGLTF).

While glancing through a news article featuring the National Gay and Lesbian Task Force (NGLTF) from a small newspaper in Idaho, I noticed a shocking example of bias.

The article was a feature story about Will Perkins, leader of Colorado for Family Values—a group that spearheaded the anti-gay ballot initiative, Amendment 2. The article freely used the terms special rights, pro-homosexuality measures and quotas, all without quotations or definitions. These phrases and words are widely recognized as loaded terms spun by anti-gay Far Right operatives to mislead people about the nature of gay and lesbian equal rights. It also referred to spokespeople at NGLTF as "extremists."

The article was written by Dirk Johnson, a widely respected *New York Times* reporter in Denver who had covered gay issues extensively and was fairly sophisticated about loaded language used by the Right. The Idaho paper apparently pulled it off the Times news wire. Before contacting the Idaho newspaper I faxed the article to Johnson, whom I had spoken with in the past. Johnson called me immediately, embarrassed and angry that his byline appeared on such a slanted piece. While Johnson had written a feature about Will Perkins, the text that appeared in the Idaho newspaper was significantly altered by someone else.

I faxed a letter to the editor of the Idaho newspaper, outlining the biases in the news article and informing him of my conversation with Johnson. I encouraged the newspaper to exclude bias from future articles, as Idaho was about to enter its own anti-gay initiative campaign. I also informed the paper I had forwarded the article to Idaho for Human Dignity (IHD), a local civil rights group, so they could monitor potential future bias in the newspaper. I demanded a retraction of the "extremist" terminology and suggested the newspaper meet with IHD representatives. I sent carbon copies of the letter to Dirk Johnson, IHD, the editor of the *New York Times,* and the Gay and Lesbian Alliance Against Defamation.

Several weeks later, the senior editor of the Idaho newspaper called me. After he received my letter he compared the article as it appeared in the newspaper with the article originally filed by Dirk Johnson. He noted the discrepancies and approached the copy editor who was responsible for placing the Johnson story in the newspaper. While the copy editor at first denied having made any alterations, he later acknowledged adding his own editorial comment. Further research showed it was not the first time the copy editor had altered articles related to gay and lesbian issues. The senior editor informed me he had fired the copy editor. He also printed a retraction of the "extremist" comment, and assured me that his paper would cover Idaho's statewide ballot in a fair-handed manner.

After just one letter and a phone call, readers of the newspaper in Idaho may be receiving more accurate coverage of gay, lesbian and bisexual issues. Do not just complain about biased coverage—take action.

—Robin Kane

Lessons from a killing

In the fall of 1996, the San Francisco Police Review Commission held hearings on the death of Aaron Williams, an African-American man suspected of a $50 pet-store burglary who died in police custody. According to witnesses and police sources, a team of police led by Officer Marc Andaya repeatedly kicked Williams in the head and emptied three canisters of pepper spray into his face. Despite the fact that Williams was having difficulty breathing, the police finally hog-tied, gagged and left him unattended in the back of a police van, where he died.

Van Jones
Director
Bay Area Police Watch
301 Mission St., Ste. 400
San Francisco, CA 94105
(P) 415 543-9444
(F) 415 543-0296
(E) ellabaker_humanrights
@sfbayguardian.com

My organization, the Ella Baker Center for Human Rights, and our project, Bay Area Police Watch, organized around this case for two years. The following is a summary of how we changed news coverage around the case and how it affected our organizing campaign for justice for Aaron Williams.

The scene

In its first set of hearings, the police commission ruled that no "excessive force" was used, that the cops' role in beating Aaron Williams was acceptable. The police commission was able to get away with such a ruling because of the abysmal media coverage leading up to the initial hearings on the case.

The few news reports were ridiculously biased. The coverage made it look like Aaron Williams had not been beaten to death, but died because of a strange malady: "sudden in-custody death syndrome." That's how the *San Francisco Chronicle* (4/8/96), the Bay area's leading daily newspaper, described a phenomenon in which victims of police beatings inexplicably die, rather than as a result of those beatings.

As often happens in coverage of police brutality, news reports during the hearings focused on the background and alleged misdeeds of the victim. In Williams' case, coverage focused on his alleged drug problem and referred to him as a parolee. There was virtually no mention of Officer Andaya's record, a man who had 37 prior complaints of police brutality, five lawsuits alleging racism and abuse and one other death of an unarmed man of color on his record.

Examining the message

After we lost the initial hearings we brought in We Interrupt This Message, a media organization that specializes in working with groups that face media stereotypes and biased coverage. They asked us to tell them what our initial media message and organizing goal had been.

Our initial media message had been: "the San Francisco police department is out of control." Not even the progressive press wanted to cover the story with that message.

The problem was that our original message forced people to be *completely* critical of the San Francisco police department in order to agree that police officers shouldn't beat an unarmed man to death. People in the neighborhoods with experience of police brutality might agree with that message. But what about people from communities that rarely suffer from police brutality?

What we were asking people to agree with us about was not particularly radical at all. Most people agree that cops should not beat unarmed people to death. So we focused on that.

We had defined our goal as justice for Aaron Williams and his family. As a media message that was too vague. When Interrupt's Kim Deterline asked us what "justice for Aaron" would look like—i.e., what we really wanted the police commission to do—we said, "Fire Marc Andaya." She responded, "Say that."

Like most grassroots groups, we knew exactly what our organizing goal was. We just didn't think we could say it to the media. We were thinking of media as separate from, rather than in support of, our organizing effort.

Strategic challenges

The next step was to look at the strategic media challenges ahead. Given the biased media coverage so far, the Ella Baker Center faced three challenges in achieving good coverage for the second round of hearings on the case. We had to rehumanize Aaron Williams, shift the focus from Williams to Andaya and establish institutional accountability for what happened.

We had to rehumanize Williams because he had been demonized in the press. We had to rehumanize Aaron so people who had heard about the case through the media could see him as something besides some crackhead parolee who happened to die, and realize the loss to Aaron's family and the community as a whole. We said Aaron Williams may not be a saint, but he did not deserve to die.

Next, we had to shift the frame and the focus of the story from the background and history of Aaron Williams, the victim, to the past misdeeds of Marc Andaya, the perpetrator. Shifting the focus of coverage to Andaya's background and record—where it should have been in the first place—was key to changing public opinion on the case.

Finally, we also had to establish institutional accountability for the police brutality that was happening in our communities. We had to put a name and a face to who was responsible for what happened in that neighborhood. And we needed to turn the tables and hold the police commission accountable for letting cops get away with murder.

Sharpening the target

We had to find a way to talk about Marc Andaya that let people know he was a racist cop and a bad apple from the beginning. So we called him a name that was becoming synonymous with racist cops: We said, "Marc Andaya is the Bay area's Mark Fuhrman."

Since the police commission had the power to fire Andaya and they were appointed by the mayor, we came up with a much sharper target: Mayor Willie Brown's police commission. We started putting it in terms of "Willie Brown's police commission is protecting the Bay area's Mark Fuhrman. If Willie Brown's police commission doesn't fire Marc Andaya, Aaron Williams' blood is on Willie Brown's hands."

The community turns out, the pressure turns up

Our media strategy became integrated with our organizing campaign. Our primary tactic was to stop business-as-usual at the police commission, bringing 100 to 200 people to every police commission meeting and having the media there to broadcast it. This constantly ratcheted up the pressure on the police commission and on Mayor Brown to do something.

Brown, who had been in the background, was suddenly in the hot seat. Andaya, who had been presented as a nice police officer who unfortunately had somebody die on him with a strange malady, became what he was: a menace and a terror to the African-American community. And Aaron Williams, who had been portrayed as some black crackhead who happened to die, became a valued member of a community and part of a family that was devastated by his loss.

Victory for the community

In a four-week period we got close to two hours of television coverage. The story went from being buried straight to the front page. And it made the front page repeatedly for several weeks. We also shifted the coverage dramatically. Both the *San Francisco Chronicle* and the *Examiner* editorialized against the police commission for refusing to fire Marc Andaya. The coverage's focus went from Aaron Williams' background, to Marc Andaya's record, to the institutional factors that allow police brutality to happen—proving that you can use an individual story to talk about institutional issues.

But more importantly for our communities, we collapsed the inept police commission. By the time the campaign was over, all three of the commissioners who had initially sided with Andaya had been removed or had quit because of the tidal wave of media and community pressure. And as a result of unprecedented community pressure, Marc Andaya was fired.

On the day that Marc Andaya was finally kicked out of the police department, the major stations interviewed Williams' aunt. Her voice broke when she said, "Now I can go to my nephew's grave…and tell him we got some justice for him." For Aaron Williams and the thousands of police brutality victims across the country, reframing media coverage is a prerequisite to any kind of justice.

—Van Jones

A previous version of this piece was published in the May/June 1998 issue of Extra!*, a bimonthly magazine of media criticism published by FAIR, the media watch group. Van Jones is director of the Ella Baker Center for Human Rights in California.*

Media crisis management

Sometimes you cannot predict a media crisis. All hell may break loose: a scathing exposé is published, a media event you are sponsoring goes haywire, a scandal erupts or your spokesperson is discovered to have major skeletons in her or his closet.

For example, who can forget the media event one inner-city community organization staged that turned into a nightmare? The idea was to sponsor a community "tag wall" for local graffiti artists to show their work and communicate an anti-gang, pro-youth, pro-community solidarity message. Unfortunately, during the event—which attracted throngs of reporters—some local loose-cannon gang decided to stage a drive-by shooting on a rival gang. Needless to say, the press covered the shooting and folded it into the story: "Anti-Gang Event Turns Violent." Yet quick-thinking community representatives were able to turn the story around. They argued: "This is precisely why we need more community resources and outreach for our youth." But they first had to face a media meltdown. What about the story of the executive director who disappeared with half an organization's budget? Or the media "poster child" who turned out to be a convicted felon? Or the anti-immigrant, right-wing politician who hired an "illegal alien" for a nanny? All of these pose media crises that must be addressed.

Planning for chaos

The best you can do is be prepared. Anticipate a crisis and be ready for controversy. Without being paranoid, you can implement some safeguards and strategies:

■ Establish clear channels of communication with the media so staff and others know their roles.

■ Create a "rapid-response team" that is charged with analyzing the situation, getting the facts and crafting the messages. This team can be comprised of key program and executive staff, as well as board members. Mobilize the team in response to a crisis.

■ Have a system in place to brief key players—including staff—about the emergency. Do not keep folks in the dark.

When the crisis breaks

Here are some tips for managing a crisis underway:

■ Do not panic. Remain calm and focused. Express concern, but appear composed, poised and professional.

■ Get the facts. Assess the impact of the controversy on your organization—the players, the numbers and the details. Present these facts to reporters to insure that all articles are factually accurate. Reporters will appreciate your openness to fix the problem and state the facts.

■ Do not ignore the crisis or pretend there is no problem. Acknowledge the situation. Then try to turn it around to your advantage by pointing out how your organization will "get to the bottom of the story so it can continue to serve the community." If possible, use the crisis to move your key messages.

- Respond quickly. The media abhors a vacuum and will fill it with other information. Do not spend an endless amount of time reviewing every detail before making a statement. At some point before the next deadline cycle, make a statement.
- Release the statement. It should be quotable and should contain your facts and your messages.
- If cameras and microphones are shoved in your face and you simply cannot say anything because you do not know what is happening, express your concern, announce your plan to uncover the facts and fix any problem, and reinforce your primary messages.
- Some information may be off-limits, such as legally sensitive data or confidential personnel matters. In this case, say something like: "Our lawyers have advised us not to speak to this issue while it is being litigated out of fairness to all parties. But what we can say is that our group is here to serve our community and deeply respects the trust and faith placed in us." Then hope for the best. Whatever you do: DO NOT SAY "NO COMMENT."
- Centralize the flow of information. Do not have numerous people speaking to different reporters. Take command of the situation. Discipline the message.
- Immediately communicate the messages to the staff and brief them on the handling of all reporters. If one person is designated to speak on the issue, have all inquiries go to that one person.
- Work with the media and accommodate them. Reporters and members of the community will generally react favorably to your honest and forthright efforts. The good will of the community and your integrity are paramount.
- Brief key allied community leaders, officials, lawmakers and clergy on your situation and communicate your messages to them.
- If your group is, in fact, wrong, apologize, announce how the problem will be fixed and then communicate a positive message about your group.
- Finally, remember the remedy for bad press is good press. Once the dust has settled and the problem fixed, come out proactively swinging and make more news.

Media meltdown

The following example is a good case study in how one organization used an out-of-control media debacle to advance their agenda and communicate their messages. It offers lessons in tenacity, careful planning, proactive action, and trusting your instincts. Most important, it illustrates the importance of framing issues and disciplining messages.

The event was the "Critical Mass" bike rally held in San Francisco. Other cities sponsor their own rallies. But San Francisco remains the mother Mass—and one particular Mass turned out to be a media meltdown, inflamed by rhetoric from the mayor and a hostile police force. It received media coverage worldwide. But if this organization could turn around this debacle, nothing is impossible!

—Seeta Peña Gangadharan

The scene

For the last six years, bicyclists have gathered in downtown San Francisco on the last Friday of every month to bike in solidarity. After the June 1997 Critical Mass ride—which exceeded 2,000 riders—the mayor declared that cyclists were "out of control," and promised to crack down on the rides.

Niko Letunic
Baytrail Planner
San Francisco Bicycle Coalition
1095 Market St., Ste. 215
San Francisco, CA 94103
(P) 415 431-BIKE
(E) sfbc@igc.org
www.igc.org/sfbc

Sensing a potentially explosive news story, the local media reported the mayor's comments widely—fixating on the image of "law-breaking anarchists." Our organization, the San Francisco Bicycle Coalition (SFBC)—a local advocacy group that promotes bicycling for everyday transportation—was concerned with the inflammatory, one-sided coverage, but we also recognized the opportunity to advance our cause.

Moving the message

With cyclists facing hostile publicity, the SFBC launched an aggressive, unapologetic anti-backlash campaign with the help of two volunteer media consultants, including the SPIN Project. We first needed to clearly set our goals: 1) educate the public about bicycle transportation; 2) obtain improvements in bicycling conditions; and 3) increase the SFBC's membership. We wanted to reframe the issue so it wasn't about "bicycle anarchy," but about "alternative transportation."

Following the aforementioned June ride, we issued media advisories, made ourselves readily available to the media and held a press conference in front of City Hall on the eve of the July Critical Mass showdown between police and bicyclists. Most importantly, we asked the nearly 1,000 members of SFBC to participate in the July ride. This escalated the conflict and drew the attention of the national media.

Because Critical Mass has no organizers, the media turned to the SFBC for the cyclists' perspective. This offered us the chance we needed to convey our messages, but also required a delicate balancing act of distancing ourselves from Critical Mass. Officially, our messages were: 1) Critical Mass was an expression of frustration with bicycling conditions; 2) The city had failed to provide a balanced transportation system; and 3) Bicycle commuting was beneficial for the city.

A media mess turned around

The actual Critical Mass did not disappoint in terms of being a spectacle—especially the way the media covered it. Numerous arrests were made, many on camera. Even some of the journalists were arrested by the out-of-control police! Irate car drivers caught in traffic shook their fists and flipped the finger at bicyclists. All was photographed by the local papers. Wayward bike-riders running stoplights were dutifully reported as if they were causing a national scandal. Radio and TV publicized the debacle live all over the world, and local and national print media featured the event prominently.

But despite the media nightmare, we *were* able to jam the coverage with our messages—mainly that lack of planning regarding alternative transportation is the problem, not the bicycle riders. And those messages repeatedly reached national prime time audiences. SFBC spokespeople were quoted in magazines and newspapers, as well as on national TV and radio shows.

The media did not stop voicing anti-bicycling messages altogether. Images of police officers arresting bicyclists not obeying traffic rules were prominently featured. But at least the coverage became more balanced and our issues were no longer invisible. As our message got out, our demands for safer cycling conditions reframed the issue and we were invited into the mayor's office for negotiations. Recognizing a losing fight, the mayor agreed to progress in several areas of importance to the SFBC.

A year later, city politicians and residents are far better educated about and supportive of bicycle transportation. Many bike-related improvements are now underway. Moreover, SFBC's membership has nearly doubled. We are now a far stronger organization.

Our experience showed us the importance of doing strategic, proactive media work. Had we not obtained outside advice from media consultants, gone on the offensive, mobilized our supporters, worked to reframe the issue presented by the other side, welcomed even negative publicity and stayed focused on a few basic messages in the midst of a media blitz, we would not have been able to advance our agenda or strengthen our organization.

—Niko Letunic

5. Media and community

Spinning for our rights
Media and your community

Proactive media activism gives you an opportunity to involve members of your community and bring them into your media plan. When conceiving your media plan, consider the role of members in your community.

In this section we look at several models for mobilizing communities through the media.

You can use your media plan to engage the community, train them, make their voices heard directly and organize them to turn out for actions and other activities. The following are some key points to consider when it comes to involving members of your community in your media action.

Media plan = organizing opportunity

If your group has an organizing plan—perhaps around a referendum, legislative battle, education campaign or community outreach program—fold media into the plan. Make sure the media people are working close with the organizing people. Identify local community media—including people of color press, campus media, community access cable, notice boards at the local co-op and neighborhood newsletters. Publicize organizing meetings, calls to action and other news about your campaign in community media.

Identify and train spokespeople

Another place where your organizing and media plans intersect is in fostering the ability of your constituents to be effective community leaders and spokespersons. Who in your community has emerged as strong, charismatic media spokespersons? Here at the SPIN Project we believe it is important to diversify the list of spokespersons so the same one or two people are not always seen in the press. That is why we encourage media trainings for community leaders. Not only does it give organizations a richer, more diverse list of spokespeople to draw from, but it strengthens the character and communication skills of new leaders in our communities.

Bringing together organizing, lobbying, research, education and fundraising

The best, most strategic media efforts bring together several components of work your organization undertakes, including: research, policy advocacy, fundraising, litigation, public education and community organizing.

This section offers case studies in (a) holding media more accountable to the diversity of opinions and voices in your community; and (b) involving your community in your media work. That means you must work closely with others in your group, including community organizers, researchers, lobbyists and fundraisers to make certain the entire machine is directed toward a common goal.

Community Organizing: Members of your community can have specific roles in your media plan, as this section details. Work closely with your organizers on the front lines of the community to ensure this piece of your media plan is successful.

Policy Advocacy/Lobbying: Your key policy people, including lobbyists, electoral strategists, program directors and select board members, will have a role in your media efforts. First, they may be called upon to be spokespersons themselves and therefore must be the "messengers" for your message. Second, the work they do may make news itself, including launching new legislative battles or political campaigns. Third, they help you set your media goals within the broader context of your political goals (for example, "Make reproductive health care more accessible to women of color" — equals broader goal — "by passing Bill XYZ" — equals strategic goal. "To do this we will have to reach key politicians through the media by making the voices of their constituents heard in

Rally/press conference/media event

Your organizing plan may call for a dramatic event to cap the year's outreach efforts. Use the media to publicize the event to turn folks out and report on the event itself, thus emboldening community members who attended. Remember, bigger crowds make better photo ops and more lively media events (*see "Case study: Lessons for a killing," page 92*).

Media briefings

As you have already learned, briefing the media on your news in advance is an important part of your media plan (see "*Organizing successful media briefings and editorial board reviews,*" page 56). As you decide who to take along to the briefing, consider inviting key community folks. Do not invite everyone. Focus on one or two people who have been trained and who represent the personal, human-interest angle of a story and/or are community leaders. Reporters will appreciate the effort to help them identify additional sources for stories.

Letters to the editor

Letters to the editor can keep the story alive in the days and weeks after it first appears. Plus they give community members a direct way of voicing their opinion. They can also challenge a media outlet's biased and indifferent coverage. Encourage members of your community to write letters (*see "Opinion editorials and letters to the editor," page 71*).

Media monitoring

Some members of the community are media "junkies." They watch every news show and read every newspaper. We call these beloved people "clip rats." They are the media watchdog warriors armed with scissors, VCRs and a comfortable chair in front of the TV set and who can monitor coverage. Nothing gets by them when it comes to watching how the media covers a story. Identify select folks who you can depend on to monitor the media and tape or photocopy articles. Divide up the list of local radio, TV and print media; assign folks to each. The clips they provide will be invaluable when it comes to responding to media coverage or building up your clip file.

> **Letters tip**
>
> Set up a letters to the editor "tree" in which select community members are asked to write a letter and notify three other people to write one as well—each of them notifying three others to write and so forth—until a bag full of letters arrives in the newsroom. The letters drive can be triggered by one or two phone calls to letter writers at the "top" of the tree, who subsequently notify everyone else below them. Provide the key messages or a suggested boiler-plate or standardized letter, but encourage writers to add a personal piece so it does not look like a form letter.

the capital through the press" — equals media goal).

Research: The folks who do issue research for you, often your policy advocates and lobbyists, will be a valuable piece of your media efforts. The work they do may result in a groundbreaking report that can be used to make news (*see "Releasing reports" on page 69*). They may also be called on to be the "experts" on an issue in the press.

Litigation: If your groups does legal work that must be a key part of your media efforts. Lawsuits and cases filed can be news stories themselves and represent a specific strategy of your organizing and advocacy goals.

Public Education: In some ways, media work is public education. But education efforts, such as instructing neighbors how to check for contaminants, or informing them of controversial economic factors, dovetail with media efforts in more specific ways. Besides sending newsletters and other mailings, or holding informative meetings or door-to-door campaigns, you must engage the media to communicate the messages of your education campaign to a wider community audience (e.g., everyone in town) or a more specific strategic audience (e.g., people over 35 years old in town). Media can help you do this and accomplish the goals of your public education campaign.

Fundraising: Your media can influence your fundraising by making your organization more visible and rallying more people to your cause. Groups that score significant media attention often report dramatic increases in membership (*see case study on the San Francisco Bicycle Coalition, page 96*). Also, your major donors and foundation supporters will delight in receiving highlighted copies of your media hits. These reinforce the feeling they are contributing to an organization that is making a difference.

Grassroots or astroturf?

Seeta Peña Gangadharan

Some corporations are co-opting the style of public campaigning and education that grassroots activists use to get their points of view across. This frequently is called "astroturfing." Corporations hire PR firms to create the false image of a popular movement around a controversial issue and use this illusion of populist support to influence policy. What community and issue-based groups do is called "grassroots organizing." For corporations and special interest groups it is "astroturfing": fake and manufactured community support. The overall effect is large corporations stand to profit handsomely by "fronting" or mimicking community-based actions.

Often astroturfing efforts are reported as legitimate community news by the media, especially if reporters do not know the difference or if authentic grassroots activists are not visible or accessible to media.

Sound insidious? Here are a couple of examples to get you thinking about the threat of astroturfing.

According to independent researchers Mark Megalli and Andy Friedman, the Alliance to Keep Americans Working, the Alliance for Responsible Policy, Citizens for a Sound Economy and the Council for Solid Waste Solutions are all names of corporate front groups whose financial support comes from Dow Chemical. Chevron, Exxon, Amoco, DuPont, Proctor and Gamble, Ford and Philip Morris are other examples of large companies that donate to a wide array of front groups.

Megalli and Friedman also found that the American Council for Science and Health (ACSH) has received funds from the likes of Burger King, Coca-Cola, PepsiCo, NutraSweet, Nestle USA and a bevy of chemical, oil and pharmaceutical companies. A primary goal of ACSH centers on placing its executive director into the mass media to defend petrochemical groups, support the nutritional value of fast foods and advocate the safety of growth hormones for dairy cows, pesticides and saccharin.

The National Smoker's Alliance (NSA) was created by the PR firm Burson-Marsteller under the financial assistance of Philip Morris, according to a study done by the investigative journalist

John Stauber. NSA actively coordinates letter-writing campaigns, organizes petitions on ballot initiatives, lobbies against smoking restrictions at state and national levels and solicits legal assistance for pro-smoking causes. It also inveighs against reporters who scrutinize the tobacco industry.

Ken Silverstein, author of *Washington on Ten Million a Day*, (Common Courage Press, 1998) writes that The Advancement of Sound Science Coalition (TASSC) was created by the lobby shop APCO Associates. With clientele in the tobacco, drug and insurance industries, APCO organized TASSC to combat the "consequences of inappropriate science...focusing attention on current examples of unsound government research used to guide policy decisions." This so-called public interest group works to develop a strong media presence, helping its members place op-eds on such items as the "hyperbolic" public reaction to pesticide use.

Yet masquerading—the essence of astroturfing—comes with a hefty price tag. PR firms are charging enormous amounts of money to mastermind corporate front groups. When this happens phony grassroots organizations become "moles of opposition," as journalist Sharon Beder once commented. "Image triumphs and truth becomes a casualty."

Because astroturfing poses a serious threat to community activists working for social change, corporate front groups must be effectively challenged.

But how do you spot corporate astroturfing? Nose around. Investigate the group's Web site, request informational material, look at the bios of spokespeople for industry connections, put in calls to an office to see if it really exists. Brief reporters covering controversial issues on the corporate connections of seemingly "grassroots" representatives.

As for your best defense—or offense, as the case may be— nothing can take the place of real grassroots representatives. Make sure your citizen spokespeople are available, articulate, and "on message," and remind reporters that you represent the real grassroots. Be accessible to reporters by developing professional relationships with them and establishing your integrity. That way, if front groups come to your town, you can expose the worms beneath the astroturf.

A community response

For years the farm-working community of Chualar has tried to get the attention of officials in Monterey County, California—but to little avail. The people of Chualar are primarily poor immigrants who have been ignored and neglected by large agricultural interests that dominate local politics—that is, until the SPIN Project and some concerned local residents decided to publicize their plight. They discovered the media is not innately adverse to their message, they just needed to learn how to tell our story.

This is the story of the how the media "discovered" Chualar.   —*Seeta Peña Gangadharan*

The problem
Chualar, a farm-working ghetto of 900 people not far from the affluent towns of Carmel and Monterey Bay, has lived with nitrate-contaminated water for more than two years, leaving residents without water to drink. This toxic water can lead to death for small infants, the sick and the elderly, and has been linked to cancer, birth defects and other health concerns. Chualar's few public facilities are in need of repair. There are no parks, only one school and the sewage facilities operate at 175 percent—thus spewing raw sewage into the earth. The largely migrant community suffers from political marginalization in Monterey County. Language barriers, poverty and race have contributed to this situation.

When out-of-town developer Priske-Jones proposed controversial developments to eventually increase the size of Chualar fivefold, news coverage focused on everything except the health and well-being of the people of Chualar. The residents of Chualar were never interviewed or consulted, much less considered, about everything from low-income housing to land-use issues.

What had to be done
It was important to the people of Chualar to bring issues of their endangered health and general quality of life to light. The prevailing media frames had to be expanded enough to include the stories of the people of Chualar. To do this, the concerned residents of Chualar had to be organized, trained and politicized.

Plan of action
We had a five-point action plan:
1. Collect and analyze all media coverage of Chualar.
2. Determine the right frame and strategic messages.
3. Determine a media strategy.
4. Identify, organize and train concerned citizens.
5. Identify all relevant media at the local, regional and national levels, including print, television, radio and electronic media.

Strategy
We planned a community and press briefing at the local elementary school to highlight the health crisis in Chualar. Each member of our 12-person group was assigned a specific, manageable task. These tasks included: contacting all English and Spanish media, coordinating the physical event, booking panel members, making T-shirts and creating visual displays for photo opportunities.

The forum
As the media arrived they were signed in, given press kits and shown to a press seating area. On the walls were posted informative charts, pictures and quotes that bolstered our frame—*"Would this ever happen in Carmel?"* Correspondents from the local ABC, NBC, CBS, Fox and Univision affiliates, as well as reporters and photographers from the main newspapers from San Francisco to San Jose to Monterey were in attendance.

Our panel consisted of three candidates for the board of supervisors who would represent Chualar, one sympathetic candidate from another district, the mayor of a neighboring city, a spokeswoman for the Mothers of Chualar, a local ad hoc group, and most importantly, an audience of Chualar's mothers and children wearing T-shirts that demanded "Clean Water Now!" Following a brief introduction, each panel member spoke for a couple of minutes. While the candidates spoke, members of our group kept our issues at the forefront by shouting catchy sound-bites. The candidates quickly retreated, but more importantly, the press knew who to film, photograph and interview. The spokeswoman of the Mothers of Chualar concluded the panel discussion with an emotional speech filled with soundbites.

After the panel, the floor was opened to the public, allowing the attendant mothers with children to plead their case before the TV cameras.

This portion gave voice to the true heart of the forum.

The aftermath

The forum received live, lead-story coverage on at least two major newscasts at 5 p.m., and was featured on all local newscasts on the day of the forum at 5, 6 and 10 p.m.

The following day, the story ran on the front page of the main local papers and continued to be shown on TV news. Less than one month after the event, the story was on TV news 45 times from San Francisco to Monterey and has persisted in the press from Sacramento to St. Louis. Moreover, the frame of the story has remained relatively consistent with our efforts to expand the frame and include the concerns of Chualar's farm-working community.

What worked well

Three things worked particularly well for us:
1. The language of the media advisory, press release and press kit were effectively geared toward the media's interests. This was reflected in all coverage.
2. The visuals conveyed our message well. T-shirts, signs and banners appeared in all coverage.
3. The staged forum was an excellent vehicle for our message, providing great photo opportunities and soundbites.

What to do better

In the future, we should have fewer people contacting the media earlier. At the same time, we should also establish a central contact for the media to call. Having too many people contacting the media makes it both confusing for reporters and difficult to manage. In addition, while we did get considerable coverage of our issue, we still need to diversify the types of media covering our issue. In the future we need to better target radio and magazine outlets as well as better reach out to news wires, including AP. We must collect and archive all coverage as well.

A look at good coverage

San Francisco Chronicle, May 12, 1998.
We got the lead story with two photographs and a perfect headline: "Nitrate-Laced Water Sickens Town." In interviews with the reporter, we were able to keep him focused on our message. This was evident from how much of our message, and our soundbites, made it into the article.

The article began with a quote from the spokeswoman of the Mothers of Chualar, a welcome change from the usual "official" sources. Her quote conveyed exactly what we wanted the news to cover—that the water was affecting her health and the health of her newborn. The story goes on to implicate agriculture as the culprit, an angle we had never seen in the local press that is normally dominated by agricultural interests.

Throughout the article the reporter reiterated our core issues: contaminated water, health risks and negligence on the part of the County of Monterey. The article ends with a quote from a sympathetic "official," who distilled the issues into an incisive condemnation of the situation.

Follow-up

Though we received tremendous media coverage following the briefing, the story could not end there. It was critical that our issues be kept alive and that the county was monitored for its reactions and responses. Thus far, the county seems to have made some effort to address Chualar's contaminated water. However, we must continue to confirm whether these efforts are genuine or merely token gestures to avoid additional negative press. Through statements to the press and additional media-oriented events, we have kept up the pressure and tried to ensure that all of Chualar's needs are met.

Concluding thoughts

When we set out on our media campaign, we never thought we would encounter the success we did. It is inspiring to see people who are consistently disregarded garner attention through such a powerful vehicle as the press. Recognizing the power of the media, however, we cannot be deluded. Success is not just coverage. True success would be if Monterey County agreed to fix Chualar's problems. Sadly, this does not seem imminent.

We cannot sit idly by, waiting for the county to do something or the media to keep the story alive. We need to be proactive and keep the story visible. This is the task at hand.

—Michael Katz

Don't forget rural media

Marcy Westerling

ACCESS to the media is critical when looking at affordable and effective ways to reach a broad number of people. Rural media markets are often ignored in the effort to speak to many people through a larger urban media. Including rural media in a respectful way will maximize your communication to more people, especially those who may want to help on your issue.

Know the media reality of the community you want to reach. This is an important rule no matter where you live or who you are trying to target. A smaller rural media culture may exist separate from or in conjunction with a larger media market. In other rural communities, there will be no large media market, just a sequence of small markets.

Know your small town market

The first step is to assess how local folks and their neighbors get their global news and their community news. How do they know when the Kiwanis will meet? Who won the last little league game? When the city will sponsor the fall clean-up day?

Marcy Westerling
Oregon Rural Organizing Project
P.O. Box 1350
Scappoose, OR 97056-1350
(P) 503 543-8417
(F) 503 543-8419
(E) ropoffice@columbia-center.org

Often the most genuine media market of the community—the one people listen to—is the one with this local information.

Include print, cable, radio and television in your analysis of how information is distributed in a community. Do not focus only on circulation figures of newspapers. The media market of my home county serves a total of 37,000 people located in five different population seats. The print market includes five local papers plus a statewide paper. Of the five locals, one is monthly, two are weekly, one is biweekly, one daily and none covers the entire population base. To reach the maximum number of people in the community, we need to access all of these sources.

Scrutinize the actual content of the media sources that cover a community. What stories are generally on the front page? Are they national political stories made local, for example, the effect of Clinton's tax plan on area businesses? Are they all human interest stories, such as "Family moves and lost dog tracks them down"? Do they have a local political/economic focus? Or maybe the paper is 95 percent sports.

Most local papers have a consistent bias toward certain stories. Once you know the angle that has appeal, you can better predict how to market your stories for local media value. Similarly, you can quickly get a sense of the political inclination of the paper. This is helpful information as you select and prepare a team of activists to approach the local editor. In a paper that only covers sports events as news, an approach to media coverage as well as communicating to the community might be to take your message to a sporting event—respectfully, of course.

The scale of rural media

The actual mechanisms of effective press work do not vary much with the media source, rural or urban: The scale does. Talk to your local press contacts about the scale on which their operation functions. Do not be surprised if it is much smaller than urban media.

For example, my first press effort with a rural media market included a press conference. The only reason any press attended was to laugh at the absurdity: Local media does not have teams of reporters to cover media events all over the county. Had I first developed press contacts, I would have known that our media market did not include staffing to cover non-sporting events. Most smaller media sources operate with a few staff covering everything.

What to send small town media

Your media submissions should be prepared to become the actual story. If the quality is good, it may be reprinted verbatim—namely because the paper does not have the staff to cover the story. Photographs and captions accompanying your release will be welcome for those media outlets that run pictures.

The press release should prove the who, what, where, when and why with quotes and background information that communicate a self-contained news story. Always include local contacts with numbers that work both day and night. If a representative from the media is not able to cover the actual event, follow up with a friendly update to confirm how newsworthy the event was.

Media briefings at the grocery store

The wonder of local media is access. Probably everyone in town knows the editor of the local paper and can easily schedule a meeting or plan an informal caucus in the aisle of the grocery store.

In one small community, the local editor was overtly homophobic and conservative—as was the paper content week after week. The local activist selected to work with the editor to turn around the coverage—in preparation for an upcoming vote on a local anti-gay initiative—started three months in advance. The activist launched a slow, methodical personal campaign that focused on maintaining a relationship with the editor while providing access to new and accurate information on homosexuality, oppression and the impact of both on the local community. The campaign started in front of the local grocery store, escalated several days later at the post office, included mini-briefings at church, and concluded months later with a dense three-column editorial asking the community to vote no on the anti-gay initiative.

While informal briefings may be easier to access, do not give up on efforts to schedule regular meetings with the staff of the paper. You might want to try and market the idea as a casual but scheduled lunch date. (In the best case scenario, such lunches would become routine.) If there is an issue that you care about but suspect the staff may be unfamiliar with, offer a lunch date to share some interesting information. Prior to the meeting, practice framing the issue for how it impacts your local community. Make sure the initial emissaries to your media are well chosen—it might be a team with criteria, including being articulate, being respected and being committed to your local group's mission.

If you live in a small town

Many of us who live in rural areas underuse the press. Either we turn to them only when we need to communicate something major, or we limit ourselves to the letters-to-the-editor page. The media can be a major tool to communicate to our rural communities. Press releases that are published equal free media attention.

Try to think about media whenever your group does something. For example, one rural human dignity group just adopted its long-term mission statement and designated a new steering committee comprised of local residents. This seemed worthy of a press release. It actually became the front page story in one of the local papers! Two weeks later the same group submitted another press release featuring the sale of bumper stickers, which also got coverage.

Another human dignity group that was not having strong community participation considered the creation of an event just to get out their name. They decided to clean up the garden of the local battered women's center. Their efforts scored positive media coverage. Another group proposed quarterly "Dignity Advocate" awards—a great way to honor a local community member and get ongoing press.

It is critical to create a system that supports rural media. Some systems that have worked well for rural-based, all-volunteer, human dignity groups include the establishment of a media team. The media team is assigned responsibility to integrate media work—writing press releases, preping spokespeople, establishing reporter contacts, visiting the editor—into every component of the group's work.

It's about hope

Rural and small-town media are restricted by tiny budgets, compared to the media conglomerate-owned, big city papers, and a focus on local news. They need support in reporting how the agenda of the Religious Right and exploitative corporations threaten the local community, and how the achievement of a participatory democracy—nurtured by the media—offers hope to the community.

Ellen in Birmingham:
A community rises

This case study demonstrates how one community turned around a bad media experience—in this case, censorship on local TV—and used it to garner more coverage for their issue.

April 1997 was a month when the nation's attention was focused on a watershed event in lesbian and gay history. The "coming out" of Ellen Degeneres and her fictional television character Ellen Morgan was possibly the biggest news on the popular culture radar screen. This is the story about how the news was not so good in one part of America—Birmingham, Alabama—and how one community turned the controversy around through the media.

Cathy Renna
Director of Community Relations
Gay and Lesbian Alliance Against Defamation
1875 Connecticut Ave
Washington, DC 20009
(P) 202 986-1360
(F) 202 667-0902
(E) glaad@glaad.org
www.glaad.org

Ellen became the first major actress to come out on the cover of *Time*, on *Prime Time Live* with Diane Sawyer and in myriad other media outlets that picked up the story. After months of hype Ellen's became the most scrutinized coming out in history—celebrity or not. And it had a national impact like none other.

Ironically, the biggest story of Ellen's coming out happened far from Hollywood, somewhere we least expected it: Birmingham, Alabama. In a unique and fascinating series of events, activists and community members came together to stand up to an egregious act of homophobia and create history—the largest gay and lesbian event in Alabama history, to be exact.

As the air date of the coming out episode (April 30, 1997) approached, the Gay & Lesbian Alliance Against Defamation (GLAAD) saw itself thrust into the national spotlight through its "Ellen Coming Out Parties" organized around the country, as well as its other work with the media. One afternoon in the beginning of April, we received a call from the Birmingham Pride Alliance (BPA), a small, fledgling community group. Jerry Heilman, general manager of their local ABC affiliate, ABC 33/40, which services more than six million viewers from Birmingham to Anniston, Alabama, had decided not to air the coming out episode. "Not appropriate for families," said Heilman. "Not what people in Birmingham want to see."

GLAAD swung into action upon receiving the agitated call from BPA, who wanted any help we could provide in this media meltdown emergency. In a matter of hours, GLAAD provided a mechanism for distributing media releases, over-the phone media training, message development, media strategy and any other technical assistance we could offer to local activists already feeling the glare of the media spotlight.

And as the days wore on, the controversy only got bigger. Within a week, local organizers debated community response, finally taking enormous personal and financial risks by leasing the Boutwell Auditorium, a popular 5,000 seat arena in downtown Birmingham, with plans to air the censored show on the day of its broadcast. By now the local, state and national media were all onto the story. A veritable media frenzy raged in Birmingham. We sent two staff people down to work with local activists to help ensure a successful event and to somehow manage the press.

Though laptops, pagers, faxes, cellular phones and other systems were installed, the key factor was the spirit, courage and determination of the Birmingham activists. They were more than willing to give up their own time, money and energy to use this situation to educate, inform and, in the words of one local resident, "put Birmingham on the gay map."

As April 30 loomed a mere week away, we worked around the clock—shaping a message that would resonate beyond the lesbian and gay community. We reached out to the "Magic City" in a variety of ways: from appearing on television and radio, to handing out invitations and flyers in gay bars, restaurants and throughout downtown. In a surprising show of support, the local country western station, WWJZ, aired round-the-clock commercials touting the public airing of the Ellen show. Local and national figures were interviewed on a daily basis. The leader of the local gay group, Kevin Snow, made a brilliant media presence (he is a stand-up comedian by trade) and helped bring this story to the forefront of media attention. "ABC 33/40 has taken away the remote control from over 6 million Alabamans, but not for long," Snow quipped on television, radio and in print.

The *Birmingham Post-Herald* began covering the story daily, a first for any local gay and lesbian issue. Local affiliate stations, gleeful at the possibility of needling their ABC competitor, covered the story with gusto. We were, as the saying goes, "everywhere." The story went ballistic, locally and nationally.

Ellen Degeneres herself referenced the spectacle in Birmingham in an appearance on *Oprah*! For media seeking a new and interesting "hook" about this television event, the Birmingham community's fight against censorship proved compelling. It was, as I remarked during a debate on MSNBC with the Reverend Jerry Falwell, "like Jerry Heilman put a lightning rod up on ABC 33/40 and drew every media outlet in the nation right to Birmingham." Lucky for us.

The evening of April 30, 1997 is one that Birmingham will not soon forget. Almost 3,000 people streamed into Boutwell Auditorium. At least 30 media interviews were conducted on-site, and *Entertainment Tonight* came to Alabama for the first time. Spontaneous marches and rallies at ABC 33/40 station erupted. The face of the gay, lesbian, bisexual and transgender community in Birmingham was forever changed. And it happened because of the media and the courage of local people. In the following months, Birmingham activists continued to talk about the impact of this event on their community—that year, their Gay Pride celebration doubled in size—on the city of Birmingham and on their personal lives.

—Cathy Renna

Conclusion

If there is one thing this guidebook has emphasized it is that your media work must not occur in a vacuum. It requires careful planning, goal setting and coordination. That is why we have saved this short piece for the last: To remind you of the synergistic, overreaching goals and tasks of your media work and how they must come together for positive social change. Your media work can bring together all the components of your struggle to make your community and country a better place to live. By proactively working with the media, you can give voice to those who are silent and a platform to those who are invisible.

Media should not be an afterthought. It should be a cornerstone of your campaign to build a justice-seeking society. A society in which no person is discriminated against because of who they are or whom they love. A nation in which economic justice is guaranteed to all. A community in which people live free of environmental poisons that harm their health. A country in which basic compassion and justice and fairness is extended to everyone. That is what is at stake in our struggle. And that is why we are spinning for our lives.

—Robert Bray

Resources

Resources for effective media strategizing by grassroots activists

The following section is designed to help activists hone their media skills—either through sharpening their knowledge of public relations work or becoming familiar with various organizations and companies that can help activists like yourself become effective media mavens.

The section is arranged in the following manner:

1. PR/media consultants
2. Media sources
3. News services
4. Public opinion research
5. Radio actualities
6. Web developers/consultants
7. Places to promote online
8. Search engines
9. Clipping services
10. Press release distribution services
11. Books, publications and Web sites
12. Groups concerned with media literacy and media bias

Please note that the SPIN Project does not officially endorse these companies.

1. PR/media consultants

As discussed elsewhere in this book, you may want to pursue the use of outside PR help when working on an intensive media campaign. Here is a comprehensive list of groups that service non-profit organizations working on social change issues. It is important to realize that some of these listings have a more national than local scope. Fenton Communications is a Washington, DC-based outfit with a large staff; Kent Communications, on the other hand, is basically a one-person operation. Whenever considering working with PR consultants, conduct background research and make sure that the group is suitable for your organization. Look at their client lists. Talk to people on staff (note: the names listed here are the principle contacts, such as presidents or executive directors). You shouldn't have a problem finding someone who can meet your needs (and budget, too!).

Cause Communications
Jason Salzman
1836 Blake #100A
Denver, CO 80202
(P) 303-292-1524
(F) 303-292-9317
(E) newsmush@netone.com
www.causecommunications.org

Communications Consortium Media Center
Kathy Bonk, Emily Tynes
1200 New York Ave., NW, Suite 300
Washington, DC 20005
(P) 202-326-8700
(F) 202-682-2154
(E) info@ccmc.org

Communication Works
Michael Shellenberger
2017 Mission Street, Suite 304
San Francisco, CA 94110
(P) 415-255-1946
(F) 415-255-1947
(E) works@igc.org
www.communicationworks.org

Fenton Communications
David Fenton, Kristen Grimm Wolf
1320 18th St. NW, 5th Floor
Washington, DC 20036
(P) 202-822-5200
(F) 202-822-4787
www.fenton.com

Kent Communications
Stephen Kent
PO Box 431
Garrison, NY 10524
(P) 914-424-8382
(F) 914-424-4849
(E) skent@kentcom.com
www.kentcom.com

McKinney & McDowell Associates
Gwen McKinney, Leila McDowell
1612 K St., NW, Ste. 904
Washington, DC 20006
(P) 202-833-9771
(F) 202-833-9770
(E) mckmcd@ix.netcom.com
www.marketing@mcandmc.com

Media Strategies, Inc.
Andrea Miller, Susan Lamontaigne
611 Broadway, Suite 206
New York, NY 10012
(P) 212-260-1520
(F) 212-260-9058
(E) mediastrat@aol.com

Millenium Communications Group
Ann Beaudry
1150 18th Street, NW, Ste. 850
Washington, DC 20036
(P) 202-872-8800
(F) 202-872-8845
(E) info@millencom.com
www.millencom.com

Miriam Zoll Communications
Miriam Zoll
PO Box 1014
Brookline Village, MA 02147
(P) 617-566-7876
(F) 617-738-1315
(E) mzoll11481@aol.com

ProMedia Public Relations
Robyn Stein
250 W. 57th #820
New York, NY 10019
(P) 212-245-0510
(F) 212-245-1889
(E) ProMediaNY@aol.com

ProMedia Public Relations (West Coast Office)
Rochelle Lefkowitz
1788 Carleton Court
Redwood City, CA 94061
(P) 650-599-9996
(F) 650-599-9998
(E) promediarl@aol.com

Public Media Center
Herbert Chao Gunther
466 Green St.
San Francisco, CA 94133
(P) 415-434-1403
(F) 415-986-6779
(E) pmc@publicmediacenter.org
www.publicmediacenter.org

Public Policy Communications
Bob Schaeffer
73 Trowbridge Street
Belmont, MA 02478
(P) 617-489-0461
(F) 617-489-6841
(E) bobschaeffer@igc.org

Riptide Communications
David Lerner
666 Broadway, Rm. 625
New York, NY 10012
(P) 212-260-5000
(F) 212-260-5191
(E) dlerner25@aol.com

The Mainstream Media Project
Mark Sommer
854 Ninth Street, Suite 203
Arcata, CA 95521
(P) 707-826-9111
(F) 707-826-9112
(E) mmp@humboldt1.com
www.mainstreammedia.org

Valerie Denney Communications
Valerie Denney
407 S. Dearborn, #1150
Chicago, IL 60605
(P) 312-408-2580
(F) 312-408-0682
(E) VDenney983@aol.com

VoxPop
Christine Triano, Jeff Gillenkirk
925 Dolores St.
San Francisco, CA 94110
(P) 415-550-0869
(F) 415-642-5473
(E) voxpop@igc.org

We Interrupt This Message
Kim Deterline, Hunter Cutting
965 Mission St., Ste. 240
San Francisco, CA 94103
(P) 415-537-9437
(F) 415-885-0563
(E) interrupt@igc.org

2. Media sources

Several companies or journalist organizations help compile media directories that can provide you with a wealth of contacts to reporters and editors. The following groups offer directories that are quite diverse, both in terms of cost and/or content. For example, many of the ethnic journalist organizations' media directories are low cost or free, provide listings of both mainstream and community ethnic press and offer information on how to contact ethnic reporters and editors at regular mainstream outlets. The more commercial services, such as News Media Yellow Book and Bacon's, are the grand-daddies of media directories, offering mostly comprehensive (not too many small or ethnic press are listed here) and extremely expensive media lists, available in a variety of formats. Both Bacon's and News Media Yellow Book may be found at your local library. Use these directories to augment your media databases whenever possible.

Asian-American Journalists Association

Member organizations directory
1765 Sutter Street, Rm. 1000
San Francisco, CA 94115
(P) 415-346-2051
(F) 415-346-6343
(E) national@aaja.org
www.aaja.org
For $50.00 you can receive listings of over 200 Asian/American-owned print and broadcast media in the U.S. on mailing labels for one-time use. Non-English language media are also included. Fax order or mail request on letterhead.

Bacon's Media Directories

332 S. Michigan Ave.
Chicago, IL 60604-4434
(P) 800-621-0561/312-922-2400
(F) 312-987-9773
www.baconsinfo.com
A two-volume media directory for newspapers, magazines, radio, and TV/cable; updated and augmented quarterly. Available in hard copy ($285/vol.) or CD-ROM ($1,395/yr); generally large public libraries and universities carry the hard copy for public reference.

Hispanic Yearbook

c/o TIYM Publishing Co., Inc.
1489 Chain Bridge Rd., Ste. 200
McLean, VA 22101
(P) 703-734-1632
(F) 703-356-0787
(E) YITM@aol.com
www.tiym.com
This annually updated and augmented resource directory contains well over 2,000 Hispanic-owned media listings in the U.S., categorized by media (print, radio and TV). The **National Association of Hispanic Journalists** at 202-662-7145 distributes surplus (but current) copies for free. Otherwise, send a check or money order for $19.95, payable to TIYM Publishing Co., Inc. There is no additional fee for shipping and handling.

National Association of Black Owned Broadcasters

Member stations directory
1333 New Hampshire Avenue, NW, Ste. 1000, Washington, DC 20036, .
(P) 202-463-8970
(F) 202-429-0657
(E) nabob@abs.net
www.nabob.org
A nationwide directory booklet of more than 180 black-owned TV/radio stations; $25.00 fee includes shipping. Each entry includes station owner and manager names, station code and con-

tact information. Fax order on letterhead.

Native American Journalists Association

Member organizations directory
1433 E. Franklin Ave., Ste. 11
Minneapolis, MN 55404-2135
(P) 612-874-8833
(F) 612-874-9007
(E) info@naja.com
www.naja.com
More than 200 print and broadcast media listings in the U.S. can be obtained in hard copy or disc format for $125.00. There is no shipping and handling fee. Order by mail by enclosing a check or money order, or fax request on letterhead; specify format desired.

National Gay and Lesbian Task Force

Queer media list
1700 Kalorama Road, NW
Washington, DC, 20005
(P) 202-332-6483
(F) 202-332-0207
(E) smindeaux@ngltf.org
www.ngltf.org
The National Gay and Lesbian Task Force regularly maintains a list of most queer media throughout the United States. Contact them directly to find out more information.

National Newspapers Publishers Association

Member organizations directory
3200 13th St., NW
Washington, DC 20010
(P) 202-588-8764
(F) 202-588-5302
(E) nnpadc@nnpa.org
www.nnpa.org.
A directory of over 300 Black-owned newspapers in the U.S. is available by either check or money order for $50.00, made payable to NNPA. There is no shipping and handling fee.

News Media Yellow Book

c/o Leadership Directory, Inc.
104 5th Avenue, 2nd Floor
New York, NY 10114-0233
(P) 212-627-4140
(F) 212-645-0931
A national news media directory, the Yellow Book includes listings of news services, newspapers, networks, TV/radio stations, programs, periodicals, international media and so on; updated and augmented quarterly. The hard copy subscription costs $290.00/, and the CD-ROM or Internet subscription costs $2,780/yr, since it provides the entire Leadership Directory, consisting of not

only news media but also government affairs, corporate, judicial and financial yellow pages, among others. There is no shipping charge for domestic orders. Most libraries and universities should carry current editions in hard copy. To order, fax request on letterhead.

3. News services

News services are a great way to cause an echo effect with the news story you're trying to get out in the public. A news service is a syndication service that supplies multiple media outlets with the same story. In this section, commercial, mainstream services, such as Associated Press, United Press International and Reuters, have been grouped with more specialized or non-mainstream services. AlterNet.org, for example, syndicates stories by independent and alternative journalists on a wire that services more than 150 alternative and independent weeklies across the nation. Pacific News Service also has an alternative bent but places its commentary mostly in print dailies. American Forum has a very specific purpose of syndicating opinion editorials or public service announcements to print and broadcast media mainly in the South. Use this list with a keen eye, and make sure you investigate exactly what type of service is being offered. Contact your local AP, Reuters or UPI office, typically located in the nearest major city.

AlterNet.org
77 Federal Street, 2nd floor
San Francisco, CA 94107
(P) 415-284-1420
(F) 415-284-1414
(E) info@alternet.org
www.alternet.org
Produces a public interest Web site offering news, features, online community and activism opportunities; and sells content to hundreds of newspapers, Web sites, and newsletters.

American Forum
1250 National Press Building
Washington, DC 20045
(P) 202-638-1431
(F) 202-638-1434
(E) forum@forum-media.org
www.forum-media.org
Distributes opinion editorials and public service announcements to mostly Southern media.

American News Service
RR1 Black Fox Road
Brattleboro, VT 05301
(P) 800-654-6397
(F) 802-254-1227
(E) ans@americannews.com
www.americannews.com
Syndicates journalism on innovative practices of individuals, communities, businesses and institutions throughout the United States.

Associated Press–National News Desk
50 Rockefeller Plaza
New York, NY 10020
(P) 212-621-1500
(F) 212-621-7520
(E)feedback@ap.org
wire.ap.org

Reuters–National News Desk
1333 H St., 6th floor
Washington, DC 20006
(P) 202-789-8015
(F) 202-371-0036
www.reuters.com

Pacific News Service
450 Mission Street, Room 204
San Francisco, CA 94105
(P) 415-438-4755
(F) 415-438-4935
(E) pacificnews@pacificnews.org
www.pacificnews.org
Syndicates articles on the wire to more than one hundred subscribing publications every weekday and sends out news alerts to news editors.

The Progressive Media Project
409 East Main Street
Madison, WI 53703
(P) 608-257-4626
(F) 608-257-3373
(E) project@progressive.org
www.progressive.org/mediaproj.htm
Solicits, edits and distributes commentary pieces to some big, but mostly small town newspapers.

United Press International–National News Desk
1510 H Street, NW
Washington, DC 20005
(P) 202-898-8000
(F) 202-898-8057
(E) feedback@upi.com
www.upi.com

4. Public opinion research

Public opinion research is something your organization might consider to help highlight your issues in the press. Below are a variety of companies that often work in the nonprofit social change arena.

Charlton Research Company
1730 Rhode Island Avenue, NW, Suite 1109
Washington, DC 20036
(P) 202-530-0010
(E) crcdc@ix.netcom.com
charltonresearch.com

EDK Associates, Inc.
101 5th Ave., 6th Floor
New York, NY 10003
(P) 212-367-7317
(F) 212-367-7517
(E) edkpoll@aol.com

Lake, Snell, Perry & Associates
1730 Rhode Island Avenue, NW, Suite 400
Washington, DC 20036
(P) 202-776-9066
(F) 202-776-9074
www.lakesnellperry.com

Peter Hart Research Associates
1724 Connecticut Avenue, NW
Washington, DC 20009
(P) 202-234-5570
(F) 202-232-8134

RIVA (Research in Values & Attitudes)
7316 Wisconsin Ave., Ste. 450
Bethesda, MD 20814
(P) 301-652-3632
(F) 301-907-0209
www.rivainc.com

5. Radio actualities

As *Making Radio Work For You!*, one of the publications in this resources list articulates *(see "Books, publications, and Web sites" page 116)*, anyone can produce a radio actuality at a reasonable price. However, if you're looking for help, the group listed below can help you with production and distribution at a reasonable price.

The January Group
1515 Jefferson Davis Hwy., #1220
Arlington, VA 22202
(P) 703-418-2060
(F) 703-418-0740

Creative Communications
2700 Hillway Drive
Boise, ID 83702
(p) 208-342-8213

6. Web Developers/Consultants

While the number of individuals and organizations helping to develop the Web presence of social change, nonprofit community remains small, things are changing quickly. Below is a short list of groups or persons who specialize in, consult on and/or design Web sites and can help your organization improve its use of new technology.

CompuMentor
89 Stillman St.
San Francisco, CA 94107
(P) 415-512-7784
(F) 415-512-9629
(E) realperson@compumentor.org
www.compumentor.org
Provides low-cost, volunteer-based computer assistance to schools and nonprofits.

Coyote Communications
P.O. Box 152473
Austin, TX 78715-2473
(P) 512-232-2295
(F) 512-232-2299
(E) jcravens@coyotecom.com
www.coyotecom.com/home.html

Impact Online
325B Forest Ave.
Palo Alto, CA 94301
(P) 650-327-1295
(F) 650-327-1395
(E) respond@impactonline.org
www.impactonline.org/services/internet
Provides "Internet 101," an introductory course on the Internet for nonprofits.

NetAction
601 Van Ness Ave., #631
San Francisco, CA 94102
(P) 415-775-8674
(F) 415-673-3813
(E) audrie@netaction.org
www.netaction.org
Provides general information about using the Internet for organizing and outreach, such as "designing effective e-mail alerts," links to technology policy sites and a list of resources for activism.

ONE-Northwest: Online Networking for the Environment
1601 2nd Avenue Suite 605
Seattle, WA 98101
(P) 206-448-1008
(F) 206-448-7222
(E) info@onenw.org
www.onenw.org
Helps conservation groups in the Pacific Northwest use e-mail, the web and other technologies in their work to protect the environment; provides equipment, consulting and training, among other services.

7. Places to promote online

Getting your story on the Web takes careful planning and effort, especially since there are not consistent standards for news online. However, there are several key places you should approach with a story idea, to run an opinion editorial or, at the very least, get a quick mention of your Web site. The listings here include places that have a specific focus, such as Corporate Watch, and broader audiences, such as the Institute for Global Communications. As the Web becomes more widely used, keep an eye out for new ones too!

Corporate Watch
P.O. Box 29344
San Francisco, CA 94129
(P) 415-561-6568
(F) 415-561-6493
(E) corpwatch@igc.org
www.corpwatch.org
Produces an online magazine and resource center documents corporate greed and provides the public with tools to investigate and analyze corporate activity.

Institute for Global Communications
P.O. Box 29904
San Francisco, CA 94129-0904
(P) 415-561-6100
(F) 415-561-6101
www.igc.org
Runs an Internet service provider with alternative sources of information for progressive individuals and organizations.

People Link
(E) people@people-link.com
www.people-link.com
Operates a Web site that helps progressive organizations and socially responsible companies communicate.

Protest.Net
(E) rabble-rouser@protest.net
www.protest.net
Lists progressive and leftist protests, meetings, and conferences worldwide, helping to resolve logistical problems that activists face in organizing events with limited resources and access to mass media.

About.com
220 East 42nd Street
24th Floor
New York, NY 10017
(P) 212-849-2000
(E) reachus@about.com
www.about.com
Offers a network of comprehensive Web sites on over 500 topics, run by expert About.com guides from across the Net and around the world.

WebActive/RealNetworks, Inc.
1111 Third Avenue, Suite 2900
Seattle, WA 98101
(P) 206-674-2700
(F) 206-674-3582
(E) webactive@prognet.com
www.webactive.com
Runs a weekly publication offering progressive activists an up-to-date resource on the web to find other organizations and individuals with similar values and interests.

Working Assets NewsBite
www.wald.com/news.html
Publishes news and columns on areas of interest to Working Assets, a progressive long distance telephone provider that donates 1 percent of profits to nonprofit organizations selected by a vote of its customers.

8. Search engines

Having your Web site listed with search engines is extremely important to developing a Web presence. If your Web site is not registered with one, then chances are your site will be overlooked by those surfing the Web. It is important to realize that different search engines employ different criteria for both registering your site with them and ranking your site. The best advice is to do occasional research on which search engines are the most popular and take into consideration their special criteria. What follows is a selective list of search engines. For a more comprehensive listing of the search engines out there, log onto www.searchenginecolossus.com.

Alta Vista
www.altavista.com

DejaNews
www.dejanews.com
Runs a search engine for finding and viewing
newsgroups.

Excite
www.excite.com

Northern Light
www.northernlight.com
Automatically categorizes findings; features an
exclusive Special Library.

Yahoo!
www.yahoo.com

9. Clipping services

Clipping services are designed to help you keep
track of your press coverage or press coverage of
an issue in which you are interested, by relieving
you of the responsibility of following your story
in the papers, on TV, over the radio and otherwise. Some clipping services are extremely expensive, and thus cost-prohibitive. Recently, free services has surfaced with the onset of Internet communications, such as Excite.com. Shoppers
beware! Some services may cost more than others.

Allen's Press Clipping Bureau
657 Mission St., Ste. 602
San Francisco, CA 94105
(P) 415-392-2353
(F) 415-362-6208
Reads more than 9,000 newspapers and 5,000
magazines in the US.

Bacon's Clipping Bureau, Bacon's Information Inc.
332 S. Michigan Ave.
Chicago, IL 60604
(P) 800-621-0561
(F) 312-922-3127
www.baconsinfo.com
Reads general- and special-interest publications
nationwide, including wire services, with the
exception of the smallest rural papers. In addition, broadcast transcripts and Internet monitoring are available.

Broadcast News eXchange
907 South Detroit, Ste. 1020
Tulsa, OK 74120
(P) 918-582-7575
(F) 918-582-8665
(E) info@bnx.com
www.bnx.com

Offers tracking reports, video clips, air checks and
news transcripts from TV stations around the
country and abroad.

Burrelle's Press Clipping Service
75 East Northfield Rd.
Livingston, NJ 07039
(P) 800-631-1160
(F) 973-992-7675
(E) info.burrelles.com
www.burrelles.com
Provides print and Web clipping, and broadcast
transcript services from media outlets nation-
wide.

Cyberscan Internet Clipping Services
(P) 310-358-0103
(F) 310-659-0361
(E) cyberscan@clippingservice.com
www.clippingservice.com
Searches and retrieves information from electronic newspapers, magazines and other publications
on the Web; also does opinion monitoring on
newsgroups and Web forums.

Luce Press Clippings
42 South Center
Mesa, AZ 85210
(P) 800-528-8226
(F) 602-834-3821
(E) clip@lucepress.com
www.lucepress.com
Reads and covers both print and broadcast media.
TV/radio transcript services are designed to com-
plement print clipping service.

Video Monitoring Services of America
330 W. 42nd St. 29th floor
New York, NY 10036
(P) 212-736-2010
(F) 212-329-5292
(E) vms@vidmon.com
www.vidmon.com
Tracks coverage ranging from segments to com-
mercials on both radio and TV, and print media
nationwide.

WebClipping.com
245 Park Avenue South, #GLH
New York, NY 10010
(P) 212-260-6627
(F) 212-260-6627
(E)info@allresearch.com
www.WebClipping.com
Searches over 30 of the largest engines on the
World Wide Web and all of the Usenet discussion
groups as well as electronic publications.

10. Press release distribution services

These services will distribute your press release to journalists to augment your media exposure, as well as decrease your workload in getting out your press release.

Internet News Bureau

(P) 541-617-5380
(E) info@newsbureau.com
www.newsbureau.com
Emails your Internet-related press release to any or all of their subscriber base of 3000 journalists.

Internet Promotion Services

410 Edmonson Circle
Nashville, TN 37211
(P) 615-832-6640
(F) 520-244-2169
(E) questions@netpromote.com
www.netpromote.com
Emails your press release to up to 2000 online and traditional media journalists.

PR News Wire

(P) 888-776-0942
(E) inquiries@prnewswire.com
www.prnewswire.com
Broadcast faxes your press release to their media contact base, or one provide them.

11. Books, publications and Web sites

The following publications will help you to better understand how the media system works both for and against you. Topics range from proactive media strategizing to grappling with media bias, and messages are aimed for both traditional activists and media activists as well. Where titles are self-published by activist organizations, the contact information for them is listed.

The Activist Cookbook: Creative Actions for a Fair Economy. Andrew

Boyd. United for a Fair Economy: Boston, MA, 1997. To obtain a copy contact:
United for a Fair Economy
37 Temple Place, 5th Floor
Boston, MA 02111
(P) 617-423-2148
(F) 617-423-0191
(E) stw@stw.org
www.stw.org

FAIR's Media Activism Kit. FAIR, New York, NY:

1998. To obtain a copy contact:
FAIR
130 West 25th St.
New York, NY, 10001
(P) 212-633-6700
(F) 212-727-7668
(E) fair@fair.org
www.fair.org

We the Media; A Citizen's Guide for Fighting for Media Democracy. Don Hazen and Julie Winokur.

The New Press: New York, NY, 1997. To obtain a copy contact:
Independent Media Institute
77 Federal St.
San Francisco, CA 94107
(P) 415-284-1420
(F) 415-284-1414
(E) info@independentmedia.org
www.independentmedia.org

Strategic Communication for Nonprofits. Larry

Kirkman and Karen Menichelli, eds. The Benton Foundation: Washington, DC, 1992. To obtain a copy, contact:
The Benton Foundation
1800 K Street NW, 2nd Floor
Washington, DC 20006
(P) 202-638-5770
(F) 202-638-5771
(E) benton@benton.org
www.benton.org

Public Opinion Polling. A Handbook for Public Interest and Citizen Advocacy Groups. Celinda C.

Lake. Island Press: Washington, DC, 1987.

Making Radio Work for You. Families USA Foun-

dation: Washington, DC, 1996. To obtain a copy, contact:
Families USA Foundation
1334 G St., NW
Washington, DC 20005
(P) 202-628-3030
(F) 202-347-2417
(E) info@familiesusa.org
www.familiesusa.org

MediaNet

www.supportcenter.org/medianet
An online tutorial covering media topics in online and traditional media.

PR Web
923 Powell Ave SW 18-3
Renton, WA 98055
(P) 425-793-9225
(F) 425-793-9230
(E) david@prweb.com
www.prweb.com
In addition to providing a free database to post press releases, this site lists many PR resources and links.

Prime Time Activism. Charlotte Ryan. South End Press: Boston, Massachusetts, 1991.

How to Tell and Sell Your Story. Timothy Saasta. Center for Community Change: Washington, DC, 1997. To obtain a copy, contact:
Center for Community Change
1000 Wisconsin Avenue, NW
Washington, DC 20007
(P) 202-342-0567
(F) 202-333-5462

Making the News. Jason Salzman. Westview Press: Boulder, CO, 1998.

Media Advocacy and Public Health. Lawrence Wallack, et al. Sage Publications: Thousand Oaks, CA, 1993.

The Publicity Handbook. David R. Yale. NTC Business Books: Lincolnwook, IL, 1991.

SPIN Project Web site
www.spinproject.org/spin
Provides media resources, tips and tools.

12. Groups concerned with media bias and media literacy

The groups listed below seek to expose how mainstream media often mis- or underrepresents various groups and/or issues due to ethnic, gender, class or sexual orientation biases. In some cases, organizations such as Fairness and Accuracy in Reporting (FAIR) approach their analysis of media bias by looking at the whole media system and come from a tradition of media criticism. Others examine media representation of very specific issues: gay rights, freedom of speech, Religious Right, or racial identity. The distinction can make a difference, depending on how you want to build your media arsenal and approach editors or reporters with the history of media coverage of a particular issue or campaign in which you may be engaged.

Applied Research Center
3781 Broadway,
Oakland, CA 94611
(P) 510-653-3415
(F) 510-653-3427
(E) arc@arc.org
www.arc.org
Publishes ColorLines Magazine, formerly RACE-FILE, which examines coverage of ethnic minorities in mainstream press and beyond.

Berkeley Media Studies Group
2140 Shattuck Ave., Suite 804
Berkeley, CA 94704
(P) 510-204-9700
(F) 510-204-9710
(E) bmsg@bmsg.org
Works with community groups and professionals to use media to advance public health policy. Monitors, studies and analyzes media to support advocacy and education.

Center for Commercial Free Public Education
360 Grand Avenue, Suite 385
Oakland, CA 94610
(P) 510-268-1100
(F) 510-268-1277
(E) unplug@igc.apc.org
www.commercialfree.org
Serves as main clearinghouse on history and research on commercialism in public education. Protects integrity of the school day from commercialism.

CultureWatch/Data Center
464 19th Street
Oakland, CA 94612-2297
(P) 510-835-4692
(F) 510-835-3017
(E) datactr@tmn.com
www.igc.org/culturewatch
Monitors the Religious Right's political agenda and strategy.

Fairness and Accuracy in Reporting (FAIR)
130 West 25th St.
New York, NY 10001
(P) 212-633-6700
(F) 212-727-7668
(E) fair@fair.org
www.fair.org
Publishes *EXTRA!* A bi-monthly magazine of media criticism.

Gay & Lesbian Alliance Against Defamation

150 W. 26th St., Suite 503
New York, NY 10001
(P) 212-807-1700
(F) 212-807-1806
(E) glaad@glaad.org
www.glaad.org
Produces GLAADLines and GLAADAlert.

Institute for the Study of the Religious Right

P.O. 26656
Los Angeles, CA 90026
(P) 213-653-7551
(F) 213-653-1737
(E) isrr@win.net
www.ISRR.org
Supports grassroots organization against the right.

Media Alliance

814 Mission Street, Suite 205
San Francisco, CA 94103
(P) 415-546-6334
(F) 415-546-6218
(E) mapd@igc.org
www.media-alliance.org
Publishes *MediaFile*, a bi-monthly journal that covers the media work environment, media ownership and strategies for activists who want to improve news coverage.

Media Research and Action Project

Sociology Department. McGuinn Hall
Boston College
Chestnut Hill, MA 02467
(P) 617-552-8708
(F) 617-552-4283
(E) ryanc@bc.edu
www.bc.edu/mrap
Researches and monitors media for nonprofit organizations, as well as builds their media capacity with strategic media planning.

People for the American Way

2000 M St., NW, Suite 400
Washington, DC 20036
(P) 800-326-7329
(F) 202-993-2672
(E) pfaw@pfaw.org
www.pfaw.org
Monitors and opposes efforts to suppress free expression.

Political Research Associates

678 Massachusetts Ave., #205
Cambridge, MA 02139
(P) 617-661-9313
(F) 617-661-0059
(E) PublicEye@igc.apc.org
www.publiceye.org/pra/
Operates a leading clearinghouse for info on political extremists.

Rocky Mountain Media Watch

P.O. Box 18858
Denver, CA 80218
(P) 303-832-7558
(F) 303-832-7558
(E) paulklite@idcomm.com
www.bigmedia.org
Studies and analyzes local TV news to help citizens and the media understand and visualize what constitutes better journalism.

Index